STILL THOUGHTS
VOLUME TWO

By Dharma Master Cheng Yen

Translated by Liu King-pong
English Edited by Douglas Shaw

Translated by Liu King-pong
English edited by Douglas Shaw
Artist: Chang Su-hua
Cover Design: Chang Shih-ming

Published by the Tzu Chi Cultural Publishing Co.
Foreign Language Publications Department
Editor-in-chief: Liu King-pong
19, Alley 7, Lane 217, Sec.3, Zhongxiao East Rd., Taipei, Taiwan
Telephone: 886-2-2898-9000
Fax: 886-2-2898-9889

Second edition, December 1996
Fifteenth printing August 2005
ISBN: 957-8300-48-4

JINGSI PUBLICATIONS
http ://www.jingsi.com.tw

Contents

Preface   vi
About Master Cheng Yen   viii

Part 1: The Dawn of Still Thoughts

Chapter 1:   Let Life Be Like a Spring Day   3
Chapter 2:   The Beginning of Success   7
Chapter 3:   A Clear Spring in a Desert   11
Chapter 4:   The Personification of Mercy and Wisdom   15
Chapter 5:   We Came Naked Into the World   21
Chapter 6:   Love Can Be Dangerous   25
Chapter 7:   Actions Are Worth More Than Words   31
Chapter 8:   The Proper Way to Manage Finances   45
Chapter 9:   Light a Lamp in the Dark   49
Chapter 10: Facing the Wind and Rain   59
Chapter 11: Healthy Yet Useless   65
Chapter 12: Many Grains of Rice Make a Bushel   67
Chapter 13: Life With a Venomous Snake   71
Chapter 14: A Knife in the Heart   77
Chapter 15: Do Not Plant Weeds of Ignorance   81
Chapter 16: A Sutra We Must Read   89
Chapter 17: March to Life's Tune   95
Chapter 18: Human Needs Will Never Change   103
Chapter 19: A Spiritual Antibody   107
Chapter 20: Drawing Water From the Ocean   111

Chapter 21: Spiritual Relief   117
Chapter 22: Sprinkle a Drop of Sweet Dew   121
Chapter 23: Bearing the Trials of Life   127
Chapter 24: We Come and Go Empty-Handed   133
Chapter 25: The Enormous Power of Compassion   137
Chapter 26: Drink the Water of Wisdom   143
Chapter 27: Let Everyone Smile   149
Chapter 28: Life Is Short   153
Chapter 29: The Place to Study Buddhist Teachings   157

Part 2: Questions and Answers

Section 1: Human Affairs

Love   162
Mothers-in-Law   179
Illness   182
One's Mindset   188
Life   197
Tolerating Insults   199
Compassion   201
Daily Affairs   205
Learning   212
Doing Work   214
Worries   219
Desires   222
Social Customs   224

Section 2: Religion

Cause and Effect	228
Eliminating Disaster	231
Superstition	232
Faith	234
Behaving Like Buddha	238
Unselfish Giving	242
Moral Cultivation	244
Karmic Hindrances	257
Becoming a Buddhist	260

Preface

In the thirty years since Tzu Chi was founded, the organization has increased from the original thirty members to four million today. Whenever I think of the Tzu Chi members, both in Taiwan and abroad, who abide by the principles of sincerity, integrity, trust and honesty, and who are engaged in the mission of helping the poor and educating the rich, my heart is full of gratitude.

In the last thirty years, many people have asked for my advice concerning all their problems. I have done my best to give them my suggestions. I have always believed that all living beings have the buddha-nature and their own innate wisdom. However, this wisdom is blocked by the poisons of greed, anger and delusion, as well as all other kinds of ignorance and worry. It is like trying to look into a mirror covered with dust.

I am grateful that people trust, love and support me. Their doubts are often dispelled and the evil thoughts in their hearts swept away by a couple of words from me. Actually, from my conversations with others, I have also received many valuable experiences and insights into life. I have compiled and edited these talks throughout the years into *Still Thoughts*.

The first and second volumes of the revised English edition of *Still Thoughts* will soon be published. I have especially asked the members of the Foreign Language Publications Department to do their best to use plain, simple English to edit these two books. Westerners who are not familiar with Buddhism may also understand the meaning contained in these books, and perhaps they may also receive a few insights.

Cheng Yen
October 15, 1996
Tzu Chi Cultural Center, Taipei

About Master Cheng Yen

Wang Chin-yun, now known as Master Cheng Yen, was born on May 14, 1937, in Chingshui, a small town in central Taiwan. Ever since she was young, the Master liked to engage in deep contemplation, asking where life came from, where people went when they died, and what people lived for.

When Master Cheng Yen was about 23 years old, her father died suddenly of a cerebral hemorrhage. Grief-stricken, she went to the temple every day and she began to think about becoming a nun. This was not an easy decision, since she was the oldest child in her family, her mother was in poor health and her younger brothers and sisters needed to be taken care of.

At the temple, Master Cheng Yen met a nun, Master Hsiu Tao, who became her mentor. Wandering wherever karma would lead them, Master Cheng Yen and Master Hsiu Tao stayed at several temples on the east coast of Taiwan. In 1961, this area was desolate and undeveloped and the people were poor. So, in a rather revolutionary break from Buddhist tradition, Master Cheng Yen and Master Hsiu Tao, believing that humans had enough suffering, firmly decided not to accept any donations from the local people. They raised their own vegetables, and earned some money by doing odd jobs, such as knitting sweaters and sewing baby shoes. In the winter of 1962, Master Cheng Yen affirmed her decision to become a Buddhist nun by shaving her head herself, a very untraditional act.

One day in 1966, Master Cheng Yen went to see a sick follower at a hospital in Hualien. At the hospital, she saw a pool of blood on the floor. People walked past it, not caring at all. Surprised, she asked, "Why is there a pool of blood on the floor?" Someone told her that an aboriginal woman living in the mountains had had a miscarriage, so the family walked eight hours to carry her to the hospital. When they got there, the hospital required an NT$8,000 [then US$200] deposit fee before surgery could be performed. The woman did not have any money, and the hospital did not want to take a risk either, so her family had no choice but to carry her back home.

When the Master heard this, she felt very sad. She wondered whether the woman would live or die, and whether her return would cost one life or two. And all because of the money. An overwhelming sadness arose in her heart. At that moment, she decided to establish a charity foundation to help the poor and educate the rich, because the poor lack material goods and the rich lack spiritual nourishment.

The Master began her work by asking each of her thirty followers, mostly housewives, to save fifty cents [US$0.02] from their daily grocery money. She fashioned little savings banks from pieces of bamboo and asked them to put the money in the banks before going to the market each day. With the motto of "fifty cents can also save people," word quickly got around every market in Hualien. More and more people participated and the program gathered strength. On March 24, 1966, the Buddhist Compassion Relief Tzu Chi Foundation was formally established. And thus a group of housewives carrying their grocery bags wrote down the first page in the history of Tzu Chi.

The work of helping the poor has developed on a broad scale. To this day, volunteers visit the homes of poor and sick people to cheer them up and see if they need food or money. Every month at the Abode of Still Thoughts in Hualien, Master Cheng Yen and her disciples distribute food to the poor. In the past three decades, Tzu Chi has helped more than one million people, both in Taiwan and abroad, and has distributed over US$68 million.

In 1979, Master Cheng Yen decided to build a hospital. At that time, she had nothing. Everybody told her that it was impossible. But she had the heart of the Great Vow Bodhisattva, who said, "If I don't go to hell to save other souls, who will?" This gave her great strength to do the impossible. The work of raising funds was difficult at first, but Tzu Chi finally received support from people at all levels of society. The Buddhist Tzu Chi General Hospital was finally completed on August 17, 1986. It was the first hospital in Taiwan that did not require a deposit fee and that directly admitted all emergency patients. Whether patients had money or not, they could receive prompt, professional medical care. Furthermore, the doctors, nurses, patients, and volunteers are like close family members. The mutual trust.and sincerity between doctors and patients and the Master's principle of "great mercy even to strangers and great compassion for all" have made the hospital Eastern Taiwan's most moving legend of modern times.

Since then, Tzu Chi has also established a Junior College of Nursing and a College of Medicine to train caring, compassionate doctors and nurses. Master Cheng Yen does not only want good, skillful doctors. She also wants conscientious doctors who will treat patients for their illnesses and at the same time respect and care for them as they would their own relatives. So, in the College of Medicine, humanitarian studies are put on the same level as the medical courses. Tzu Chi has also established the Tzu Chi Taiwan Marrow Donor Registry, which now has the world's third largest data bank of volunteer marrow donors. Cooperation agreements with other registries in the world are being established in order to share information and increase the chances of finding a donor match.

The Tzu Chi Foundation continues to look ahead to the future. The foundation is currently planning to construct a disabled children's rehabilitation center in Northern Taiwan and a Tzu Chi branch hospital in Southern Taiwan. Tzu Chi is also planning to establish Tzu Chi University, which will be based on the College of Medicine, and which will include colleges of liberal arts, management, religion, and fine arts.

Buddha taught that religion transcends race, nationality, and geographical distance. Tzu Chi first began international relief work in the spring of 1991, when members went to help victims of a typhoon in Bangladesh. Since then, Tzu Chi has also helped victims of war and natural disasters in China, Mongolia, Ethiopia, Rwanda, Cherchen, Nepal, Cambodia, Thailand, South Africa and Guinea-Bissau.

Part 1
The Dawn of
Still Thoughts

1
Let Life Be Like a Spring Day

The Goal of Life

❉ Wherever we go, there is always a starting point and a goal. We should pursue our goals from the very beginning till the very end, never stopping halfway along the journey. It is more tiring, and even dangerous, to struggle in place in the middle of the road than it is to progress toward reaching the final goal. Mountain climbing is a fitting example. You must either stand at the bottom of the mountain or climb continuously to the very top. By stopping halfway up the mountain, you put yourself in danger of being hit by falling rocks.

❉ In our lives, we will always encounter unfavorable situations, times of foggy or chilly weather that bring discomfort. If we remain committed to our goals, it will be like warm sunshine in winter.

❉ Life is filled with changes, but wisdom endures forever. Love is boundless, and the spirit persists forever.

A so-called profession is only a job for earning money. You punch the clock and try to complete your assignments on time in the office. But the work of Tzu Chi has nothing to do with being on or off duty. At every moment in your life, you must remain committed to your mission.

Doing good deeds always takes time. This is the goal and the obligation for your life.

Life lasts but a few decades, whereas wisdom is eternal. Just as we give life to our children, we should also provide them with wonderful memories and an education in love. In this way, we can make our wisdom immortal.

4/11/07

Those who become Buddhists must have a goal, while those who lead others to Buddhism must be responsible. As one navigates across the sea of life, one must have a goal. This is the goal of becoming a Buddhist. One who leads others to Buddhism is like a person who sees that a ship is about to go astray and quickly lights a lamp in a lighthouse to let that ship know the way. This is being responsible.

 To be fully alive, you must continuously utilize your capabilities, talents, and intelligence for others. Your life must be like a spring day, constantly radiating vitality. Do not let your conscience hibernate.

 The reason the world, the nation, society and families cannot achieve a peaceful and friendly state is because we only fight to survive, but fail to discover the significance of survival.

2
The Beginning of Success

Perseverance

- Commitment is the starting point of success. Human life needs commitment and hope in order to achieve any success. All buddhas achieve the goal of becoming a buddha by first being committed and then practicing their commitment. Without commitment there cannot be hope, and without hope we can accomplish nothing.

- Buddhism puts equal emphasis on commitment and action. If we sit and talk idly but never put our commitments into action, we will never fulfill them.

- We must make commitments that are beneficial to all living beings, and we must always and everywhere realize them in action.

- In order to save all beings, we need to be committed and show care and concern for all creatures.

✠ We must be committed and perseverant; we must be gentle and prudent.

3
A Clear Spring in a Desert
The Spirit of Religion

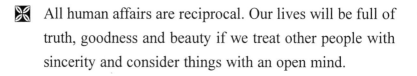 Some people do not understand the teachings of Buddha. They assume that only those who are facing big troubles need religion to resolve their problems. To them, Buddhism appears to be passive and escapist. This, of course, is incorrect. People who have knowledge and virtue and who are determined to explore the true meaning of the universe and the mysteries of life also need religion, especially Buddhism.

All human affairs are reciprocal. Our lives will be full of truth, goodness and beauty if we treat other people with sincerity and consider things with an open mind.

The true spirit of Buddhism lies in unselfishness. We should do everything possible to make all living creatures peaceful and happy. We should sacrifice our own interests and work hard for others.

✠ To be a Buddhist, you must have the perseverance of a marathon-runner. You can only reach the finish line, buddhahood, if you are willing to run.

✠ Only religion can encourage us and help us to be reborn.

✠ To be really free, we must have a religious spirit and a true goal in life.

✠ If you want to have an other-worldly spirit to do this-worldly affairs, you must maintain absolute perseverance, absolute diligence, absolute forbearance, absolute love, absolute happiness. This is the "absolutism" of the Buddhist spirit, which is different from the "relativism" of this world. It is also the essence of leading a perfect state of benefitting all creatures.

✦ A true Buddhist will not only worship Buddha, but will imitate Buddha as well. He will try to imitate Buddha's great wisdom and mercy.

✦ Buddhist teachings can be an effective medicine for curing life's diseases. All creatures in the world share the same sufferings. Natural or manmade disasters are all caused by physical and mental disharmony. It is the teachings of Buddha that can bring us to a state of harmony, both physically and spiritually.

4
The Personification
of Mercy and
Wisdom
The Heart of a Bodhisattva

We should select our religious belief with a rational heart and then pursue that belief under the guidance of truth. Each of us has a bodhisattva's heart, which possesses the qualities of mercy and wisdom. These are the good qualities of a bodhisattva, as well as of our very human nature.

A bodhisattva is a merciful person, one who is constantly concerned for the welfare of all creatures. Wherever he goes, he never feels frightened. If we can treat others with love and compassion, we will never offend others and will always get along well with others.

A bodhisattva's compassion is boundless, broad enough to accommodate the entire universe. He extends his love to all beings, asking nothing in return. Therefore, he is content with what he has and, unlike ordinary people, wants only wisdom.

- Each one of us has the buddha-nature. If we can activate our conscience and altruism, all of us can save and benefit other people. This saving heart is the heart of a bodhisattva.

- If you want to be a bodhisattva, you must undergo spiritual trials and tribulations. You must be brave enough to face hard work, cultivate unwavering perseverance, and bravely strive toward your goal of redeeming the world.

- The love of a bodhisattva is like a glass of water. It is clean and colorless. You can see all the way through it from the very top to the very bottom. It is a love as pure as clean water.

- A bodhisattva is not a carved wooden image. A real bodhisattva is a kind person who can work, speak and eat.

✠ You must be determined to reach the goal of becoming a bodhisattva. A bodhisattva will do what he has to do, no matter how difficult it is, and he will do so as happily as if he were playing a game.

✠ To a bodhisattva, life is but a play performed on a stage. We are all actors or actresses playing different roles on the stage of life.

✠ The value of life lies in what you do, not in what you look like. The image you project does not have any value at all.

✠ We should be happy for the accomplishments of others. It is a bodhisattva's mindset to regard others' achievements as his own. We will live happily when we always strive to be kind and helpful to all living beings.

- The wooden and stone buddhas and bodhisattvas in temples are not the real Buddha that can inspire us. They merely help calm us so we can concentrate our minds on the study of the teachings of Buddha. The truly inspiring Buddha can only be found in our hearts.

- We must face challenges bravely if we want to walk on the Path of the Bodhisattvas. When we meet troubles or dangers, we must maintain the fearless, unflinching perseverance of Buddha. We must courageously go forward and never turn back.

5
We Came Naked
Into the World
Making Good Use of Our Bodies

✸ We should cherish our bodies, since they can help us do good deeds. We must make good use of our bodies, for all our achievements are accumulated gradually through bodily actions.

✸ We cannot avoid the life cycle of birth, aging, illness and death. We cannot escape the suffering of illness. Buddha said, "I am a good doctor. I can diagnose and prescribe for a patient. But it is beyond my ability to determine whether he will listen to me or not." If you know that you are sick, you must listen to the doctor's advice to treat your illness.

✸ We came naked into the world. After decades of hard work, we can take nothing with us. Life is just that simple: we come and we go empty-handed.

✠ Loitering away each day turns us into consumers of life. Only by working energetically can we become creators of life. We waste our lives when we live idly. We can make them much more enjoyable by being kind and helpful to others.

✠ There are generally two ways people treat their bodies. You can love it too much, as if it were too valuable to be utilized. Or, you can despise it excessively, as if it were too filthy to be cared for. However, if you make good use of your body, you can achieve great things and realize the teachings of Buddha.

✠ Make good use of your body while you can to help others, promote the teachings of Buddha, and lead others to goodness.

As disciples of Buddha, we should imitate the spirit of Buddha by helping others and sharing their happiness and troubles. A successful, meaningful life can only be realized if we are concerned with other people.

6
Love Can Be Dangerous
Love and Romance

※ If a person indulges in excessive self-love, he can hardly avoid conflicts with others. He thinks that others are making fun of him, and he is afraid of what they might do to him. Being so suspicious and insecure, he feels that his life is only misery.

※ A loving, merciful, compassionate heart is the mark of a woman. It is a wife's duty to guide her husband in the right direction, and it is a mother's duty to do things that are beneficial to others.

※ To practice the teachings of Buddha on earth, we must work to purify others. But before we try to purify the hearts of others, we must first purify our own. What is purification? It means to cultivate the pure love of Buddha. And what is the love of Buddha? It means to love all living beings in the world without asking for anything in return.

✠ If you want to lead and inspire others, you must first light up your heart. A true leader must be sincere and hard-working, not just capable. You must accommodate others with an open heart and give your love to all living beings.

✠ There is a common disease in today's society: loveless-ness. If we can first start with ourselves and fill our own hearts with love, and then give that love to each other, then everyone will be filled with love and society will be harmonious.

✠ A river of love can be as dangerous as a tidal wave; an ocean of lust can be as treacherous as a hurricane. It is painful when you fail to attract the one you love, yet it is even more unbearably painful when you succumb easily to other temptations after winning the one you love.

✠ Some people only look after the members of their own families. But people of this sort become upset easily when family members fail to meet expectations.

✠ The desires of ordinary people can never be satisfied. The desires for material comforts and carnal pleasures in life are like waves, coming one after another. This is the source of unhappiness.

✠ Love is boundless. If you give love unselfishly, it can be beneficial to all creatures. But if you keep it totally for yourself, it can create bad karma.

✠ The divorce rate for the middle-aged in Taiwan is rising rapidly, causing numerous problems for our society. We should first nurture healthy family ethics in our own homes before we can help other families.

- You need to cultivate a good relationship with your spouse every day. Even if the relationship turns sour, you must take one step backward to accept reality with an open heart. Love the person that your spouse loves [sic], and it will be a great love.

- It is fortunate to be a loving person and to be loved by another. But our love for others should be pure and undefiled. A person who gives love should ask nothing in return, and the recipient of love should not be greedy. In this way, both the giver and the receiver can dwell happily and freely.

- When we break the limits of our love, extend it to all living beings, and regard their suffering as our own suffering, this is the kind of love that Buddhism talks about.

True love does not distinguish time, place, religion or race. No matter when or where people are suffering, if we can see, hear and reach them, we should do our best to help them without asking for anything in return. We should offer our pure love even to people with whom we do not have a special relationship, and we should have the compassion to share in the unhappiness of others.

We should strive to imitate Buddha's love for all living beings. What Buddha could do, we can do. Buddha could love, and so can we. Since Buddha sacrificed his life in order to love all beings, we should devote our time and energy to achieving our mission of helping all living beings.

7
Actions Are Worth More Than Words
Moral Cultivation

The reason why a man has two ears, two eyes, two hands and two feet, yet only one mouth, is because he should listen, observe and work more, but say only a little. A Chinese philosopher once noted, "A frog croaking day and night is detestable, while a rooster's crowing is useful." A few significant words can carry great meaning, while meaningless prattle only makes others drowsy. It is more likely that we will achieve our goal of moral cultivation by carrying out what we have learned. Our actions are worth much more than our words.

 Moral cultivation actually means refining one's personality and correcting one's bad behavior. One should bear in mind a sense of shame. Show me a person who does not know how to examine his soul and I will show you a person who does not possess a sense of shame. He never behaves himself well, and it is impossible to talk with him about the refinement of personality.

✠ The various methods of moral cultivation, such as meditation and the chanting of sutras, serve the function of strengthening our concentration. The purpose of moral cultivation is to get rid of your false self and allow you to be your real, true self.

✠ It is not difficult to achieve a pure society. We should start toward this goal by first doing good deeds. In order to make all of society beautiful, each of us must begin by making our own efforts. If we combine all the beauty of individual achievements, then all of society will become beautiful. If we long for the fulfilling world of a bodhisattva, then we should start to behave like a bodhisattva.

✠ We must be careful about what we are going to say. We must make sure our words will be reasonable, inspirational, and helpful.

- The effort to cultivate our virtue must be achieved through daily conduct and should be done carefully and patiently. Only by acting in accordance with the teachings of Buddha can we realize the goal of behaving like Buddha and cultivating virtue.

- How do we measure one's spiritual cultivation? It exists inside, but it is shown outwardly through daily behavior.

- Just as we all have different faces, we also have different ways of behaving. In order to cultivate our morality and practice Buddhist conduct, we must try to work and live smoothly with others. We have to get along with everyone and always treat others nicely.

- You can't be good yourself when no one else around you is good.

- A strong person is one who can tolerate insult and who cannot be knocked down by physical pain or mental anguish. Tolerance is the cornerstone of success.

- A person will never do immoral or unreasonable things if he has a strong sense of shame. When a person wants to cultivate morality and behave like Buddha, he must first cultivate a sense of shame.

- In order to practice the teachings of Buddha, we should enlighten not only ourselves, but others as well. We should constantly cultivate our wisdom and mercy, never offending or slandering others.

- In this world, we often encounter many unfriendly people and complicated matters. As we learn to deal with them, we cultivate morality and virtue.

- People often harm others for the sake of self-love. Buddha, therefore, teaches us that rule number one for reaching the goal of moral cultivation is never to harm others.

- A society's stability stems from its family education. Family education is based on personal moral cultivation. If we do a good job in moral cultivation and take good care of our families, then we will create a peaceful society.

- Those who can tolerate the faults of others are people of great fortune and intuition.

- We can never rely on others to help cultivate our morality. We can only enjoy the fruits of enlightenment by our own efforts. We should not forget: "no pain, no gain."

✠ We should always act carefully, but not narrow-mindedly, in our daily conduct.

✠ You should always keep your mind free from anxiety, cultivate healthy concepts of life, conquer worry, and shun the material desires of this world. When you have, do not be greedy for more; when you have not, do not be frustrated. This is the way to achieve mental and spiritual freedom.

✠ There are three important points that devotees and students of Buddhism must remember. First, you must have the pure, innocent heart of a child. An honest heart is the place for enlightenment. Second, you need to cultivate the spirited endurance of a camel. You should work as diligently and as patiently as a camel. Third, you should have the courage of a lion. Improve yourself as fearlessly as a lion.

37

If we want to accomplish anything important in the world, we must first cultivate virtue and refine our personality. Above all, we must always and everywhere respect others.

If we want to act like Buddha, we must be concerned about other people. If we discipline ourselves in the midst of daily affairs, bravely face difficulties and challenges, and always put other people first, this is the true spirit of behaving like Buddha.

When we carelessly spread nasty gossip, even though we may not be hurting others' bodies, we can sometimes damage their reputations, which is even worse. Physical pain is temporary, while ruining someone's public image may twist his personality for the rest of his life.

We must be honest and sincere when talking or doing business with others. Furthermore, our own viewpoints should be based on reason and logic when we discuss the teachings of Buddha with others. We should not tell fear-inspiring stories of miracles and mystery. Only by promoting Buddhism through a healthy, reasonable approach can we upgrade others' knowledge of Buddhism and lead them on the path to goodness.

 "Penetrating truth together" means that the Buddhist students in a group help one another enter a realm of understanding by discussing the teachings of Buddha, eliminating worldly mannerisms, and nurturing a pure and innocent heart like that of the Buddha.

 "Coursing together" means that when Buddhist students in a group make mistakes, they correct each other and admonish each other.

You who are cultivating your morality must be aware of four things in your daily conduct: your words, your behavior, your manner, and your heart.

First, to be aware of your words, each word you utter must encourage and inspire others. By doing so, you spread the Buddha's teachings.

Second, to be aware of your behavior, act respectably in your daily conduct. Your behavior will reveal your virtue.

Third, to be aware of your manner, you should always be dignified yet gentle when dealing with others. People will like to be near you, and they will never look down on you. Confucius once said, "Be gentle yet serious, be authoritative yet not too rude."

Fourth, to be aware of your heart, you should be tolerant and cheerful. Constantly cultivate a heart of joy, delight in helping everyone, and be thoughtful towards others. In this way, everyone will be happy.

❊ We must always bear one rule in mind: we must act justly and righteously for the sake of Buddhism and for all living beings. We should tolerate others' misunderstandings and unfair accusation. In all things, we should be able to face ourselves without guilt.

❊ Those who want to practice the teachings of Buddha must have a tranquil mind. "When a bird flies across the sky, it will leave no trail on the white clouds. When a carp jumps out of the stream, it will draw no marks on the surface of the water." We should not worry about things that happened long ago.

❊ When a person lives in fear and anxiety, he easily loses confidence and becomes trapped in cowardice and escapism.

Abstention, contemplation and wisdom are three necessities for practicing the teachings of Buddha. Abstention means that we should not have illusions or be tempted by worldly desires, we should do our duty, and we should be able to abstain from selfishness, greed and the eagerness for fame. Contemplation means that we should remain calm and resolute when in trouble. Wisdom means that we should be able to calmly overcome difficulties.

 "Asceticism" means to purify one's heart, diminish one's worldly desires, and cultivate a strong will power to endure difficulties and challenges.

 "The saints have no dreams" is an old Chinese saying. When a saint wakes up, he lets go of all his dreams and immediately faces real life. He devotes his energy to work, not dwelling on dreams.

Before saving the world, we must first save our own hearts. A sincere heart is the basis of proper behavior. As Confucius once said, "In order to unify the world in peace, we must first cultivate ourselves, have a good family, and govern our country well." If we want to get along well with each other in our family, we must improve our own personal morality. Then, our family can be an example for others. When each family becomes harmonious, we can have a peaceful and happy society.

8
The Proper Way to
Manage Finances
Money and Finance

※ People in this world commit numberless crimes to collect treasures. There is an old Chinese saying: "The desire to obtain money is the source of trouble." To act like Buddha, we need to cultivate a heart of mercy, happiness, and courage so that we will be willing to give unselfishly. We should be clear that earthly treasures are only for giving people to live on.

※ Our wealth is like fire: in winter, it can keep you warm; but if you get too close, it can be dangerous. If you can't let go of it, it will be like holding a piece of hot iron: you will surely get burned. Worldly fame and fortune are like ice: it looks beautiful, and it can keep your tea cool in summer; but if you hold it too long in your hands, you will suffer frostbite. People are confused: they know that fame and wealth can be dangerous, yet they are willing to be hurt.

✵ For fame and wealth, most people dishonestly flatter others. You must know that it is painful when people cannot be honest with each other. If you don't want this pain, turn your greedy heart into an honest heart. Earn your money honestly and use it in meaningful activities for the good of all. In this way, you will be happy and free.

✵ You cultivate good fortune for yourself by giving to charity. If you put all your money in the bank and never use it, you will be no better than the poor. Your wealth will be meaningless. If you use your worldly wealth properly and meaningfully in this world, it will be a great opportunity to cultivate good fortune.

✵ Buddha tells us to divide our income into four portions. We can therefore spend one-fourth to support our parents, one-fourth on our children's education, another portion on family expense, and the last share on public welfare.

Money can hurt people, but it can also save people. We should use money to help others, and not be used by it. If the rich and powerful cannot learn to limit their desires, they will have nothing but unlimited anguish. If people cannot let go of fame and wealth, their spiritual lives will become corrupt and everything will be meaningless.

9
Light a Camp in the Dark

Acting Like Buddha

- People who want to act like Buddha must look at life and death clearly. If you make the most of your life and do your work well, your family and society will live in harmony. If people can get along well with each other and the environment, there will be no disasters, and people will live longer and enjoy more good fortune.

- To act like Buddha, we must first have a heart full of happiness and freedom. In order to do so, we must behave properly and reflect constantly upon our actions. We will be free after examining our conscience and finding no big mistakes.

- Both Buddha and Jesus Christ came into the world to save us and to be our models. In order to save us, they, too, had to face the realities of life and overcome many difficulties.

- In order to maintain good judgment, we should use our reason and intellect to understand the impermanence of life. All people, regardless of status or wealth, can live in peace and freedom, without concern for what they might gain or lose.

- It is merely superstition if we only believe in Buddha but do not act like Buddha. You cannot call yourself a Buddhist if you only worship Buddha. You will be acting like Buddha if you imitate Buddha's virtue, compassion and wisdom while seeking to understand yourself and the essence of the universe.

- Chinese people traditionally clean their homes and repaint their walls at Chinese New Year. For those who want to act like Buddha, every day should be like the New Year. We should constantly get rid of the old dirt in our hearts and make our hearts fresh and pure every day.

✤ Buddhists often compliment each other when they perform a good deed by saying, "Your merits are boundless." Actually, if we do good deeds promptly, without complaining, and without asking for anything in return, this is the true meaning of "boundless merits."

✤ Under the Buddhist concept of cause and effect, good fortune comes as a reward for good deeds. Wealth is not the only thing that can create good fortune. Only if we can be concerned for others, chant Buddha's name, examine ourselves and take care of others, this love will create good fortune.

✤ The most important thing for people who want to act like Buddha is to cultivate compassion. Otherwise, you will lose the spirit of Buddhism.

✵ If you can activate your true nature and sense of responsibility, then you will naturally be able to do all things easily and without complaint.

✵ We can never extend our lives of wisdom if we evade our responsibilities and live idly.

✵ In order to act like Buddha, we must thoroughly get rid of our own worries, as well as the unhappiness and hostility of others.

✵ Both Buddha and Jesus Christ came into the world to save us and to be our models. In order to save us, they, too, had to face the realities of life and overcome many difficulties.

�֎ In order to behave like Buddha, we should not only study Buddhism, but we should also concretely practice what we have learned.

✖ We must focus our concentration and make the right choice. If we keep changing our minds, we will always remain at the first step and will never be able to progress to the next step.

✖ We act like Buddha for the sake of helping all living creatures. We act sincerely toward others for the sake of getting things done readily.

✖ Acting like Buddha means fulfilling your duties, regardless of your position or work. Do not be confused by wrong concepts and overlook the fact that you are living in this world.

- Young Buddhists often immerse themselves in the reading of sutras. However, the true essence of acting like Buddha is applying the wisdom they have learned from sutras to the actions of daily life.

- When we can charitably ignore others' bad habits, praise their good qualities, and do not criticize their shortcomings, our life will be praiseworthy and enjoyable.

- Life is happiest when you are needed by others and can do things for others.

- To act like Buddha, we should start with the basic things that we can do. Do not miss any opportunities. Our merits accumulate through our daily conduct. The sooner we start to cultivate our virtue, the sooner we will see it reach fruition.

✠ Accepting Buddhist teachings means that after we have listened to the teachings of Buddha, we apply what we have learned to daily life.

✠ Before we learn to act like Buddha, we are often dominated by worldly desires, yet always feel that we are lacking something. Even when we think we have grasped something, we can never settle down. It is like putting a drop of water in a desert: the desert will still be as dry as before. Now that we have the luck to learn Buddha's teachings, we must limit our desires for material things and let go of all our attachments. We should always feel grateful and positively make the best use of our time and energy to cultivate our altruism and knowledge, thus progressing on the truly meaningful path of life.

✠ The real meaning of acting like Buddha lies in getting along well with others.

✖ Those who want to act like Buddha must keep a heart that is motivated to search for the truth. If you fail to do so, you will lose the light of wisdom and your path to the truth will be blocked. Watch out for your thoughts, and do not let what happens around you extinguish your lamp of wisdom.

✖ To learn Buddha's character, you must maintain an attitude of impartiality. You must feel equally happy towards every person you meet. When you look at others through the eyes of Buddha, everyone will be a buddha.

10
Facing the Wind and Rain

Personal Growth in a Challenging World

✠ If you constantly have difficulties, thank heaven for the good training.

✠ Very few people realize that life is filled with changes. We can hardly predict if we will be as healthy or fortunate tomorrow as we are today. People often think, "If only I had..." Many people have good intentions, but they never carry them out. It is too late to regret, and at the end of their life they feel anxious and fearful.

✠ When others criticize you, ask yourself if your conscience is clear. If so, your mind will be at ease.

✠ Do not talk too lightly about frustration or inability. You must overcome these problems, even though they may be as hard as rocks. Besides, your troubles might actually be as thin as paper.

✠ Do not complain about friction and disagreement between you and your friends. Replace the complaints with understanding, forgiveness and joy.

✠ Don't lose your commitment each time you get a little frustrated. If you have a Buddhist's courage and confidence, you will be able to face difficulties and illness with a joyful heart, because they will help you to get rid of your bad karma.

✠ Suicide is wrong for three reasons: First, a person who commits suicide destroys the body given to him by his parents. Second, suicide creates bad karma. Third, a person who commits suicide abandons his responsibilities to his parents, spouse, and children.

✠ Only by enduring the trials of life can we become great.

※ When life is easy, people tend to lose themselves. It is therefore good luck when we occasionally face setbacks and frustrations, for they wake up our consciences and help us grow.

※ We can eliminate the problems and bad karma in our lives by performing our duties well and joyfully accepting everything that comes. In all things, we must depend on ourselves. It is useless to pray to Buddha for his help. Instead, we should act like Buddha, so that we can create our own good fortune.

※ You reap what you have sown. When you are healthy, you should do good deeds for all. In this way, you will pave a road of health. When you are sick, your children can look after you, but they cannot endure the pain for you.

✠ If we joyfully accept the bad karma from our past lives, then our penance will be lighter. Even though the bad karma caused by our past sins is very long, we can end it much sooner if we endure it gladly.

✠ Feel grateful when others try to hold you back, for their doing so will help you grow stronger.

✠ Buddhists are not afraid of trouble, and they actively throw themselves into serving others. In our service to others, we must not be swayed by what happens around us, and we must courageously overcome all obstacles. We must do what others cannot do, endure what others cannot endure, and give what others cannot give. This is taking advantage of all difficulties to strengthen our minds.

11
Healthy Yet Useless
Unwilling to Walk on the Road of Justice

- A person with two hands that refuses to work is no better than a person with no hands.

- We must always walk on the road of justice. If a person only walks on the road of evil, he is more pathetic than a person with no feet.

- A devil is one who blocks the road of justice, prevents people from doing good things, and breaks their commitments. The devil outside of you is not as horrible as the one inside your heart. The inner devil can disturb your sense of peace and love so that you harm others and ruin yourself.

- If you did not have your two feet, it would only affect you personally. But if you had both feet and yet refused to walk on the road of justice, you would harm any number of people and destroy any number of families.

12
Many Grains of
Rice Make a Bushel
No Good Deed Is Too Small

✠ Many grains of rice make a bushel. If you neglect even one grain of rice because you think it is too small, how can you gather a full bushel?

✠ Boundless merits are accumulated little by little, day by day, throughout your life.

✠ The good deeds performed by many people are greater than those done by a single person. No matter how big a candle is, its light is still limited. But when one small candle can light hundreds of thousands of other candles, their light can shine everywhere.

✠ We should have self-respect, but at the same time we should be humble. None of us can single-handedly hold up the sky.

Opportunity knocks only once. We should grasp every chance to do something good, or else the chance will be gone and it will be too late. Some people want to do good deeds, but they want to wait until they have more money or time. Know that life is impermanent. When the opportunity comes, don't be afraid that you have only a little strength — just go do it. Do whatever you are capable of doing. Don't think that any good deed is too small to do.

13
Life With a
Venomous Snake

The Five Poisons of Greed, Anger, Delusion, Arrogance and Suspicion

Worry is more dangerous than an enemy. You must always be aware, and do not let your conscience fall asleep. Otherwise, your heart will be occupied by the evils of murder, robbery, debauchery and greed.

Anger hurts people by destroying their good relations with others. A momentary intolerance not only damages good reputations, but it also destroys all your past good merits. An angry heart is worse than a blazing fire. Things that are burned up by a fire can be replaced, but when a person's character has been destroyed, it cannot be bought back for any amount of money.

The invisible tornado in our hearts is ignorance. The invisible sword in our hearts is jealousy. The invisible demonic possession in our hearts is suspicion. And the invisible prison in our hearts is superstition and magic. These four can destroy the roots of goodness and demolish a forest of good deeds.

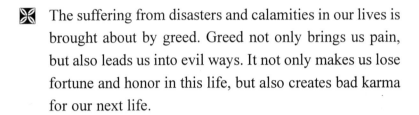 The suffering from disasters and calamities in our lives is brought about by greed. Greed not only brings us pain, but also leads us into evil ways. It not only makes us lose fortune and honor in this life, but also creates bad karma for our next life.

Greed, anger, delusion, arrogance and suspicion are the five illnesses of human beings. There are also five desires that can bring us unhappiness: the desires for wealth, sex, fame, lavish food and idle sleep. It will be easier for you to deliver yourself and other people if you remove these five desire-driven illnesses.

All the troubles of life arise from three poisons. The wars in the world, the turbulence in countries, the decadence and corruption in society, stagnation in business, breakups in personal relationships, all happen because of greed, anger and delusion.

73

Most common people tend to be greedy. When they obtain money and power, they want even more. When a man has a beautiful wife, he still wants a pretty mistress. When a woman has a good husband, she still desires to make him submissive. When their son is well-behaved, they demand that he ace every course in school. Consequently, the common people live unsatisfactory lives, forever pursuing fame, money, love and everything else. Their lives are unspeakably bitter.

Worry is like a venomous snake that will bite you if you touch it. We must eliminate senseless worry so that we can practice Buddhist virtue.

Buddhist teachings are actually very simple. You can enlighten your mind and realize the buddha-nature in your heart by eliminating greed, anger and delusion. Human beings, however, have many worries. This is why Buddha has 84,000 ways of dealing with 84,000 worries.

✳ Many people are hypocritical because of their greed. True goodness and happiness are attained by getting rid of our confusion, desires and worries.

✳ A thief in this world cannot steal everything you own. But once you become angry, the thief within your heart steals away all your merits.

✳ If you give only because you expect to gain something in return, you will create more worries. When you donate money to the poor without a sense of joyful giving, you will not gain any merit and you will only create more worries.

✳ We should view the people around us as mirrors for self-reflection, so that we can imitate their good behavior and avoid repeating their mistakes.

Most people make themselves unhappy because of their worldly desires. Their striving for fame and wealth causes any number of people to forget their moral principles and damages any number of reputations. Desire can tempt people into an abyss of worry, so desire is really the source of suffering. Therefore, we should let go of all our desires for material things and protect our consciences from being confused by our desires.

 All creatures cycle from one meaningless incarnation to the next. They only think about enjoying the present, but thus only create more bad karma. Their lives slip by unconsciously. They think that every day will be as peaceful as today. They don't realize that "the moon will not always be full, the flowers will not always be in bloom, and the beautiful scenery will not remain unchanged." They fail to realize that nothing is permanent.

14
A Knife in the Heart

Bearing Insult

- We will never be able to achieve anything great in this world if we cannot bear insults while performing our duties conscientiously. We must be able to endure all kinds of suffering in order to learn and practice the teachings of Buddha.

- Tolerance means that we joyfully accept the good and bad karma from our previous lives.

- Many people think that monks and nuns leave the world and go to far-off places to do their spiritual formation. In fact, the true spirit of leaving the world lies in accommodating all sorts of people and events and not being influenced by all that happens around you.

- The elevation of personal virtue hinges on tolerance. If everyone could tolerate insults, there would be no arguments.

- Try to maintain a tranquil mind even when you are working. In order to live happily, you must maintain your search for truth when you are busy and not let your morality fall asleep when you are relaxing.

- Tolerance is a great power that can help you do good deeds and practice Buddhism. If you can maintain tolerance, there is nothing that you cannot do.

- Be sure to keep calm and remain tolerant when you and your colleagues have dissimilar ideas or interests in the office. Watch your mouth. You must never utter an unkind word to others.

- You must have a saint's tolerance in order to attain transcendental freedom. If you fail to do so, you will never be enlightened, no matter how much you worship Buddha.

If you can tolerate others, and if others can accommodate you, then you will be truly successful.

When you are attacked or tricked by others, do not get angry, but be grateful instead. If there were no bad people, then there would be no good people. If there were no suffering, there would be no chance to show the love and tolerance of the bodhisattvas. Therefore, you should bear all insult and slander cheerfully.

15
Do Not Plant Weeds
of Ignorance
Mind

※ A joyful heart is like a springtime breeze that cheers up the people around you.

※ People's hearts are all the same. When we came into the world, we all had loving hearts like that of Sakyamuni Buddha. However, our hearts changed as we grew up in different environments and picked up different habits. Therefore, we need to cultivate virtue to restore our hearts.

※ Buddha teaches us that we can live happily if we are always content with what we have, behave properly and maintain tranquility.

※ Do not feel bad when you lose your worldly wealth. What is really tragic is to lose your inner treasure without knowing it. Everyone has the pure, true buddha-nature, but it is hidden by worries and ignorance.

We should be vigilant in times of peace, and prepared for any problem that should suddenly come by. Those who practice Buddhism must constantly train themselves to remain calm and tranquil in turbulent situations.

When we listen to others, we should listen from the speaker's viewpoint. When we listen to a young person talking, we should listen with a young person's mentality. When we listen to an old person talking, we should listen with an old person's attitude. In this way, we can maintain harmony in all situations.

Persistence breaks through all difficulties and obstacles, like dripping water that can wear away a stone.

The human mind is more destructive than lethal weapons, since the latter was created by the former.

- We must first bring our bodies and minds into harmony before we can cultivate compassion, attain wisdom, and achieve the goal of helping and leading others.

- All worldly wealth, power and fame are empty. True fortune lies in a heart full of love and compassion. You do not need to have a lot of power, prestige or wealth. With a loving heart, there is nothing that you cannot reform, nothing that you cannot guide.

- At all times, we should examine our intentions to see whether they are rooted in the desire for fame and fortune. Gradually, our hearts will be uplifted to a state of harmony and peace.

- There is no need to be afraid of submerged reefs along life's voyage if we remain sincere and devoted to the people around us.

- You will never accomplish anything if you fail to concentrate. Be sure to eliminate all random thoughts in order to have a pure, clear mind.

- Every person's heart has a piece of the Pure Land — a good nature. If we keep it free of dirt and weeds, the land will always bear the blossoms of wisdom and the fruit of enlightenment. This will not only beautify our lives, but also purify our hearts.

- If we maintain pure hearts, we will enjoy a pure world. We should protect our minds from the poisons of greed, anger and delusion. We should actively protect the world from disasters and pollution and keep society free from violence.

- We should change our greed into contentment and our contentment into compassion.

❋ If we want to remain happy, we should view human friction as a sort of education in how to get along with others and how to deal with problems.

❋ The worries in our minds are like thieves. When we are not aware, they will not only hurt ourselves, but also destroy others.

❋ If we want to remove all the disasters in this world, each of us must improve his own heart. When each of us has a healthy heart, then our society, our country and even the whole world can live together peacefully.

❋ Buddha teaches us to bring our minds and bodies into harmony. He also tells us to change our anger and hatred to love and tolerance. At every moment, we must forgive and love others.

Each of us, like Buddha himself, has a mine in our hearts that is rich in precious stones. The difference is that the Buddha's mine has already been opened and all the precious stones have been dug out and polished. Ordinary people, on the other hand, haven't opened their mines. Even if they have, they have not polished their jewels.

16
A Sutra We Must Read

Family Ethics

✻ If we want our families to be fortunate and harmonious, we should bless our families every day and always be joyful.

✻ Parents can only fulfill the duty of raising their children. However, parents cannot demand that their children grow as they want them to.

✻ Birds have their nests and people have their families. How can we enjoy family happiness when the husband, wife and children live in different places?

✻ When a husband has more than enough to eat and wear, his wife should encourage him to do good things for others and be considerate for the poor. It is also a wife's duty to be thoughtful towards her aged father-in-law and mother-in-law, so that her husband will be able to relate to his parents without friction.

✠ The way a husband and wife speak and act towards each other not only sets a concrete example for their children to follow, but also invisibly teaches them how to deal with the world.

✠ A true Buddhist family emphasizes the importance of courtesy. Courtesy is still the most beautiful attitude in life.

✠ Whatever we do, our manner must be polite, considerate and loving. We must get rid of all our self-attachments.

✠ Our bodies are composed of various material components. Therefore, illness and death are normal. I, too, suffer from illness. However, I try to bear it without complaint. Though our bodies might be physically weak, our spirits can be strong and healthy.

A family should not only seek a life of material plenty, but must also emphasize spiritual communication, so that everyone in the family can live in harmony.

When a family is in harmony, even if it is materially poor, it can still be rich in joy. Material wealth does not make up for the agony and regret of family disharmony.

I have heard many people say, "My country's social order is bad and the quality of life is deteriorating. I want to emigrate to another country." Emigration is such a tiring matter. It is equivalent to transplanting a tree in a new place. It is unpredictable whether the tree will be as sturdy as it once was. It is very hard to adapt to a new environment with a different climate and strange soil.

�֎ In my opinion, emigration is passive and a form of escapism. It is better for us to make our own home more livable than to move to a foreign country. We should become more concerned about our own country's problems, such as environmental pollution or social problems, and treat them as if they were our own personal responsibilities. It is merely a matter of time until the ugly duckling changes into a beautiful swan.

✖ Love does not make demands on others. Love gives of itself and offers without conditions.

✖ Our life is full of illness. The disharmony of our bodies is an illness, family quarrels is another, and social turmoil is a third.

17
March to Life's Tune
A Meaningful Human Life

※ To lead a truly meaningful human life, we must use our abilities to save ourselves and to save others. Otherwise, we are no better than the other creatures who need Buddha's help. When a human can help himself and help others, he no longer needs Buddha's help.

※ We should constantly reflect on what we have done in the past. If we waste our days in idleness and decadence, then we only live in confusion.

※ You will get along better with others if you behave naturally toward them. If each person thinks of himself as being normal and no better than others, than everyone will live in peace.

※ Our lives in this world will be wasted if we just fool around every day. We should always use our abilities in the spirit of the bodhisattvas to do good for others.

✠ No one is an island. We cannot live apart from other people. Wherever there are many people, there will be many different viewpoints, which often leads to friction between people. This friction must be overcome with tolerance. Tolerance will help you expand your world until it becomes as boundless as the sea and sky.

✠ People who have nothing to do are not happy. Also, there are people who do not do proper work, but only busy themselves with social activities, gambling and sightseeing. After all that, they feel exhausted and empty. They are not happy at all.

✠ When a person in this world thinks of nothing but his own life and his own desires, then his life is unimportant to others. On the other hand, if he uses his life to do good for all, then he will make himself indispensable to the world.

- Once a person becomes lazy and just idles away his time, he becomes dispirited. Life will soon become meaningless to him.

- No one can single-handedly get things done in this world. We depend on each other in order to survive. For instance, we need to wear clothes, but even if you know how to make a suit or a dress, you still need the help of the people who can supply the cloth and thread. Therefore, be grateful to those who make our existence in this world possible.

- If we just float through our lives in this world and let our bodies decay every day without doing anything significant, then our lives will be truly meaningless. Therefore, we should follow the guidance of ancient and modern philosophers and study the questions of where we come from and where we are going.

❉ It is natural to go through the life cycle of birth, aging, illness and death. Don't worry about it. It would be better to live happily each day.

❉ We will never tire of helping others if we do it voluntarily.

❉ We should not fool others with flattering words or behavior just to reach our own ends. In the end, we only hurt ourselves.

❉ Letting go of this life is not pessimistic. In fact, it is positive and optimistic. It is not that we look down on this world, but that we look through this world. It is not that we do nothing, but that we do it at the right time. It is not that we have nothing, but that we are content with what we have.

One of the most fulfilling feelings you can experience is when you do your best at this moment to do good for others.

Serve others voluntarily and without complaint, in spite of hardship and criticism. Then no matter how busy you are, you will always feel unlimited joy.

Life without love is boring and meaningless. If our love is limited only to our own families, we will hurt not only ourselves, but also other people. Therefore, we should extend our love to all living beings and ask for nothing in return. Those we love will have no pressure and will feel happy and free.

A happy life does not lie in money, power, fame and status. It is based on the love and care between people.

- Wisdom must be modest. Wisdom helps us to distinguish the good from the bad, and modesty makes our lives happier. Therefore, wisdom and modesty go hand in hand.

- If you can feel happy when others feel happy and if you can feel fortunate when others feel fortunate, then you will indeed have a contented, fortunate life.

- Life is a stage. Some people suffer their whole lives. Some suffer first and then enjoy themselves. Others first enjoy themselves and suffer later. So we say that life is impermanent. Who can decide who is the happiest? Only love lasts forever.

- People are always tossed by the currents of life's changes and caught in storms of ignorance. You must always be alert so that you can live in peace.

- Life is like a play. All the troubles of life begin and end as the curtain rises and falls, so you should not become attached to them. It is the wisdom of the bodhisattvas to replace our worries with pure compassion toward others.

- Lazy people will certainly fall into evil ways. We should always make progress in our lives, and not let the gains and losses in life make us lose our will to struggle.

18
Human Needs Will
Never Change
Service, Duty and Gratitude

✜ Our lives are short, but the universe exists forever. In the last few thousand years, there have been many changes in human history, but mankind's basic needs will never change.

✜ Those who live to serve others are not afraid of hardships and are willing to shoulder even heavier responsibilities. So long as they can help all creatures and relieve their suffering, these people are happy and seek no other reward.

✜ We should cultivate a spirit of independence. Do not rely on others for help. If we are determined, there is no burden that we cannot carry.

✜ A cultivated person will do the best he can to fulfill his duty. He does what he must do, no matter how long it takes.

※ Life is worth living when you are given great responsibility. Life will be empty and meaningless when you evade your responsibilities.

※ A person is more admirable when he is strong enough to take all responsibility.

※ Do not try to take it easy all the time and decrease your responsibility. You should try to increase your strength. With strength, you can shoulder even more responsibility.

※ If a person is always grateful and thinks about the source of his life, then he will know that we all depend upon each other for our lives. One person cannot live by himself. Therefore, we should share what we receive. Give more, help others more.

✠ Your days will be peaceful if you do not worry about gains or losses in life.

✠ Be grateful to those who receive your help, since they give you the chance to walk on the Path of the Bodhisattvas. They show us that life is bitter, empty and impermanent. How, then, can we afford to miss any chance to help others when we are healthy and secure?

✠ To get rid of our worldly desires is not enough. We need to have a heart of gratitude. When we give, we must not expect the recipients of our charity to thank us. Rather, we should thank them.

✠ Those who are in want show us how lucky we are to have what we need. Therefore, we should always be grateful to those who receive our charity.

19

A Spiritual Antibody

Confidence, Perseverance and Courage

✠ Be persistent in the midst of adversity and distress. Don't just follow the fashions of the times.

✠ With courage and confidence, nothing is impossible. The only obstacle to your success is your lack of willingness.

✠ Hard work demonstrates perseverance and endurance. So if you want to accomplish anything, you must have a spirit of hard work.

✠ Our spirits must have an antibody to become immune to the influence of the world around us. This antibody is contemplation.

✠ Our spiritual riches will make us happy, even if we are materially poor.

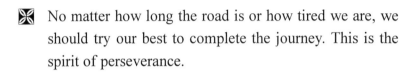 No matter how long the road is or how tired we are, we should try our best to complete the journey. This is the spirit of perseverance.

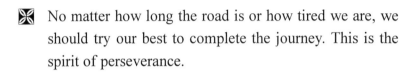 When we learn Buddhism, we must have confidence in ourselves. We should also have the courage to get rid of our worries and worldly desires, so that we can live peacefully and freely.

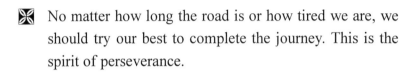 If we do not trust ourselves, we will lose our direction in life. If we do not trust others, we will not be able to establish good relations with them. It will then be difficult to accomplish anything meaningful.

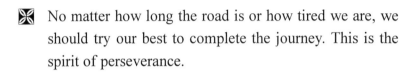 Some people idle away their lives and accomplish nothing, because they lack the confidence and courage to face reality. Weak people often have trouble dealing with others.

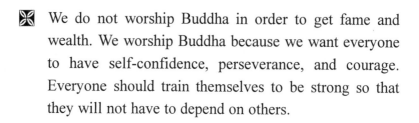 We do not worship Buddha in order to get fame and wealth. We worship Buddha because we want everyone to have self-confidence, perseverance, and courage. Everyone should train themselves to be strong so that they will not have to depend on others.

If you are willing to educate all people, make an inhumane person merciful, a jealous one tolerant, a stingy one generous, an evil one kind, then this is the wisdom and perseverance of the bodhisattvas.

20
Drawing Water
From the Ocean
Luck, Fortune and Happiness

There are four ways to acquire good fortune: incessantly carry out Buddha's teachings, be merciful, enlighten fellow humans, and calmly tolerate insults.

Those who give actually receive the most, because those who give are always more fortunate than those who receive.

Those who are fortunate should also cultivate wisdom. Spreading our love by sharing what we have with society is the way to seek good fortune and cultivate wisdom.

We should use our time and our abilities to help all living beings. When we give unselfishly to others, we will feel that our lives are real and meaningful. We will not feel that our lives have been wasted. We can thus lead a happy life.

✠ Those who give will feel peaceful and happy, while those who receive will be warm and well-fed and will feel human warmth.

✠ When disasters and troubles stay far away from you, then you are lucky. Big problems become small ones, and small problems disappear. Luck is a form of good fortune.

✠ Each of us hopes to be happy, but happiness is something that cannot be measured by material possessions. It is a spiritual feeling. If we can always feel spiritually content, we can enjoy truly happy lives.

✠ Life is filled with changes. In this world, we should not be concerned about what we lose or gain. Actually, if we have peace of mind, if we can work, and if we can enjoy what we have, then we are fortunate.

We will receive greater fortune if we become forgiving and thoughtful. That is why Buddhists say, "It is good fortune to be forgiving."

When we draw a bucket of water from the ocean, the ocean will still be there. Giving of yourself unselfishly is equivalent to drawing ocean water: no matter how much water you draw, the water level remains the same. The ocean's water level is not going to rise if you do not draw water from it. Continually giving to others is the only way to create and increase good fortune.

Wealth does not always represent good fortune. True good fortune is peacefulness.

We should always do the best we can to help others, even if we can only contribute a little. If we pool all of our efforts, we can help a lot of people.

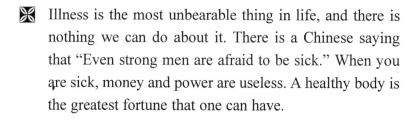 Illness is the most unbearable thing in life, and there is nothing we can do about it. There is a Chinese saying that "Even strong men are afraid to be sick." When you are sick, money and power are useless. A healthy body is the greatest fortune that one can have.

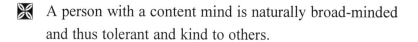 A person with a content mind is naturally broad-minded and thus tolerant and kind to others.

21
Spiritual Relief
Compassion and Wisdom

- We should help redeem people from their suffering by kindness, compassion, joy and unselfish giving. In this way, we can acquire spiritual joy and eternal freedom in our lives.

- May our compassion be spread to all living beings in every corner of the world, so that they may be as happy as if they were bathing in cool, bright moonlight.

- A compassionate person will behave gently. Compassion and gentleness can help people get rid of their worries.

- A good, kind person feels happy when others are happy, and he does things that benefit others. This is true wisdom. If a person only does things that benefit himself, he is only being clever.

- Do not look down on yourself. Every living being is as wise and compassionate as Buddha. Whatever Buddha can do, you can do.

- A "clever" person's heart is filled with thoughts, delusions and perplexities. He should wash them away with the pure water of wisdom, so that he can maintain a clear mind.

- Kindness means to always share your happiness with people around you. Compassion means to promptly help living beings that are in trouble.

- When a person is dominated by the delusion of lust, his heart will become dark. We should therefore rid ourselves of all delusion by lighting the lamp of wisdom in our hearts.

- The purpose for studying Buddhist teachings is not to be more intellectual, but to inspire wisdom. Wisdom comes from contemplation.

- We should speak gently and behave kindly, so that people around us can feel warm and happy.

- The essence of compassion is love and benevolence. We must offer our compassion to others with sincerity and kindliness.

22
Sprinkle a Drop of Sweet Dew
Less Desire and More Contentment

※ Do not worry that you may be less capable than others. Think about how you can get along with and help others. This is the way to lead a contented, happy life.

※ The things in this world are for us to use. Those who are never content lack wisdom and thus are used by the things of this world.

※ Demanding things always brings pain. If we keep demanding from others, we will gain nothing but countless worries.

※ We should be content and happy with what we have. Be thrifty, so that you can share with others. There are many people in the world who need our help. We should give what we have, money or time. In this way we can perform countless meritorious deeds.

- Mankind's worldly desires are as dry and thirsty as a desert. But Buddha's teachings are like sweet dew: they quench our thirst and wash away our desires.

- If we can reduce our desires, then we will have nothing left to worry about.

- If we want to learn to behave like Buddha, we must first get rid of our desires and learn to be content, so that we can achieve peace and wisdom.

- When someone always dresses plainly and neatly and keeps himself well-groomed, we can conclude that he lives a sincere life. On the other hand, when someone likes to show off his luxurious new clothes, we can be sure that he is a vain person who is filled with endless material desires.

※ Some people's desires can never be satisfied. When they have something, they still want more. If a person feels content with what he has, he lives in stability and happiness.

※ Unbridled lust and passion are a source of human suffering. Contentment is the only solution for this.

※ Contentment will make one's life happy and peaceful. A content person finds comfort anywhere, whereas a discontent person complains even in paradise.

※ There is little difference between a wealthy but discontent person and a poor person. A poor but content person is spiritually wealthy.

�֍ A content person will do what he can, even if it is only a
little, to offer his love for others.

�֍ The smile of a patient is the most beautiful and touching.
It is like the warm sunshine after a thunderstorm. It comforts those around him — his family, friends, doctors and
nurses.

23
Bearing the Trials of Life
The Ego

We cannot ask others to do the impossible, but we should demand this of ourselves.

Our characters should be as smooth and polished as sea-washed pebbles, rather than as rough and abrasive as stones dynamited from mountainside cliffs.

But think about it. Ask yourself: Where was I before I was born? What am I in this world? What did I really gain after arguing with others today? When am I ever really "myself"? By reflecting on these questions, you will probably discover that each "self" is but an illusion.

You should not think of yourself as being more important than others, but at the same time you should not look down on yourself. Even if you are only a tiny bolt, you must make sure that you are screwed in tightly.

It is because people put themselves at the center of their lives that there is illness and trouble in the world. People should humble themselves, as though they did not exist in this world.

 You may pretend to be stupid toward others in order to avoid arguments, but you can never fool yourself. Trying to do so wastes your time and your life.

 We should constantly examine ourselves: we may have good, loving hearts, but are we actually showing them? Think about how your words and actions may have offended others. Through constant self-examination, we avoid making big mistakes.

 If we want to truly help others get rid of their troubles, we must do so wisely according to what they really need.

※ People often forget the meaning of humility. When they understand something a little bit, they think that they are so wonderful. They always think that what they say and do is better than anyone else. They are always so egotistic.

※ The way that a person talks reveals his character and credibility. The most important thing in his relationships with others is to make himself trustworthy. He can cultivate his moral character by behaving sincerely and honestly, and by refraining from criticizing others.

※ Accepting the criticism of others is a kind of lesson. You should listen carefully and then behave prudently. You should eliminate arrogance, stubbornness and egotism, so that you can cultivate morality and conduct yourself properly.

In order to turn a piece of iron into something useful, we must melt and refine it in a furnace and then hammer and bend it into the proper shape. The chastisements we receive from others are like the hot fire in a furnace. If we can bear these trials, we will become successful people.

 We cannot demand that others act perfectly; it is better to demand perfection of ourselves. We must not demand that others change to suit us. It is better for us to adapt to others.

 People's minds are often influenced by the outside world. We happily hold our heads high when we are in favorable circumstances, only to grieve and weep when we are in trouble. A person's mind cannot remain calm if his emotions are dominated by the outside world.

24
We Come and Go Empty-Handed
Letting Go of Attachments

- The accomplishment of countless meritorious deeds eradicates countless worries. By doing so, we leave all our suffering and come to pure happiness.

- We should frequently wish ourselves luck, and we should relax and be happy.

- In order to cultivate mercy and to be filled with the joy of Buddha, we must let go of all the worries that bothered us just a minute ago.

- In this world, we cannot get away from worldly affairs. If a person maintains good relationships with others, has an open mind and optimistic personality, and performs his duties well, then he has a good perception of "worldly values."

- If a person clearly understands what the Buddha taught, and if he is not influenced by what happens around him, then we can say that he has a good perception of "real values."

- If a person is not attached to real values and is not influenced by worldly values, but brings both into harmony, then he has a good perception of "good values."

- How can we free our minds from the chains of life and death? We must cultivate the ability to let go of our attachments and obsessions.

25
The Enormous Power of Compassion
The Task of Tzu Chi

We should be constantly concerned about our Tzu Chi Association, and be brave and happy when we face challenges and difficulties. We should make the most of our lives, and combine our resources to benefit all living beings.

Tzu Chi commissioners are as compassionate as the bodhisattvas. They serve as the hands and eyes of Kuan Yin, the Goddess of Mercy, who has one thousand eyes to see the suffering people of the world and one thousand hands to help them. Through these commissioners, we can see the enormous power of compassion.

If we want to walk on the Path of the Bodhisattvas, we must endure numerous trials. If we want to be Tzu Chi members, if we want to be bodhisattvas, then we must diligently do our own work. We must overcome all difficulties one by one.

There are three prerequisites for volunteers in the Tzu Chi Hospital:

• They must endure hardship and work diligently.

• They must realize that the more they do, the happier and more energetic they will be.

• They must be gentle and relaxed. For example, if they know that a patient has cancer, they must not show their sorrow, but should be calm and relaxed and cheer him up.

 Those who have good fortune acquired from their previous lives can easily get rich in seconds. However, people who do not have that fortune can hardly save any money, no matter how hard they work. The Tzu Chi Association is like a fertile field. You plant in it the seeds of good fortune so that you can reap a fine harvest in your next life.

✠ Tzu Chi commissioners must have a charming demeanor and an elegant appearance. They must wear the spirit of Buddhism on their right shoulder and the good image of Tzu Chi on their left, and they must present a warm personality that comes directly from the heart.

✠ When you do Tzu Chi work, you must be equipped with the spirit of a loyal volunteer. You must help and encourage one another. Do not feel upset when you meet with difficulties. If you compare yourself with others objectively, you may fall short of the best, but you will be better than the worst. Commit yourself to doing good for others.

✠ Doing the work of Tzu Chi is like pushing a cart uphill. You must work hard to get all the way to the top without stopping. If you stop halfway, the cart will surely slide downhill.

- Tzu Chi's task is to inspire people's altruism. One more Tzu Chi member means one less bad person.

- The reason why society has become so disordered is that so many people have unrealistic desires for extravagant lifestyles. Tzu Chi's task is to make people more practical and let them use their free time for meaningful activities. In this way, their families will be happier and society will be more peaceful.

- In order to do good deeds, we must have good opportunities. Tzu Chi is a good opportunity for us to do good deeds on the Path of the Bodhisattvas.

- It is wiser to view society with confidence and love, rather than with worry.

26
Drink the Water of Wisdom
Deliverance, Impermanence and Progress

❋ Deliverance means to use mercy as a way to save and help others.

❋ Karma is the condition of your present life, generated by your behavior in past lives. There is a "common reward," in which people who share a common karma are born to the same race and nation. There is also an "individual reward," based on your personal karma, which determines whether you are rich or poor, beautiful or ugly, intelligent or stupid.

❋ The reason why we repeatedly chant Buddha's name for people who are about to die is to make them less frightened and give them spiritual peace. However, the chanting of Buddha's name does not guarantee that the people who are about to die will go to the Western World ["Paradise"]. If there were such a guarantee, we would not need to cultivate virtue or believe in the concept of cause and effect.

We make the seven-day Buddhist retreat in order to understand Buddhist rituals and etiquette. We should listen carefully to the lectures on Buddha's teachings and engrave them in our hearts. The retreat should help to purify our bodies, minds and words. In this way, the retreat will bring us merits.

 If we want to have good fortune, we must each learn to cherish and create good fortune first, then we can all cultivate the three great "fields of fortune." The "field of gratitude" is respect for our parents, teachers and elders. The "field of reverence" is reverence for Buddha, his teachings and his disciples. The "field of compassion" is caring for the sick, helping the poor and sympathizing with all living beings.

 If you have confidence, you can cross even the widest river. But if you lack confidence, you cannot cross even the narrowest creek.

When a person talks a lot without saying anything, we say that he is just playing with words. An articulate person's sermon on Buddhist teachings may sound good, but if what he says has no meaning for your daily life, then he is just playing with words. If a person studies Buddha's teachings, yet fails to put them into practice, he is also only playing with words.

The study of Buddha's teachings is suitable for people of all educational backgrounds. When highly educated people study the teachings of Buddha, they feel that they are deep and profound. Moderately educated people feel that Buddha's teachings are useful. Uneducated people feel that Buddha's teachings give them support.

People often become confused. They regard the impermanence of this world as permanence and unhappiness as happiness. Their minds frequently become distorted, and they end up going to hell for their bad deeds.

We can make rapid progress by controlling ourselves and constantly re-examining our behavior. We should put this good character into practice in our daily lives.

 Many Buddhists go on pilgrimages to mountains, which they respect as symbols of virtue. Along the way, these pilgrims prostrate themselves every three steps. In doing so, they are able to become enlightened by the sense of morality that exists deep in their hearts. It is not that the mountain itself is holy, but that it represents a direction and a goal for the progress of our lives. An old Chinese poem goes as follows:

You need not search long for Buddha's Spirit Mountain;
it exists no where else but in your heart;
Everyone has a pagoda on Spirit Mountain
Where he can go to cultivate virtue.
We cultivate our morality when we bring the spirit of our
pilgrimage into our daily behavior.

27
Let Everyone Smile
Preserve Life

When the plum trees are in full bloom on a cold, gloomy winter day, we feel the beauty of nature. When we offer our love and help to those in trouble, life does not seem so cruel.

It is a show of benevolence if you refuse to kill any living creature. Benevolence is a kind of love. All truth and good deeds are based on love. Love prevents us from killing or harming any life and enables us to actively protect all living beings.

A family's poverty and unhappiness is generally caused by illness. Thus, it is possible for us to help restore the family's well-being by teaching its members to take precautions against disease and by curing the sick members so they can stand up again and help shoulder family responsibilities.

A healthy, productive society must be based on the concept of mutual help and concern. When you ruin the good image of others, whether intentionally or not, it is like spitting into the wind, a gesture that only soils your own face. You can never slander others without damaging your own reputation.

 We should put ourselves in the position of others, so that we can better sympathize with all that suffer from poverty, illness and distress. We must give of our love to help them: feed those who are hungry, warm those who are cold, cure those who are sick. If we encourage all those around us to do humanitarian acts, then we truly protect life.

 Let us warm the sad, lonely hearts of others with our sincerity and eagerness to help.

Many Buddhists believe that they gain merit by taking domestic animals, such as birds, and releasing them into the wilds. This is a bad idea. To do so is to release them to a certain death, because they depend on us for their food and shelter. It is better to quickly provide assistance to those in need than to release caged animals into the wilds.

28
Life Is Short
How to Live a Fruitful Life

✠ Human life passes in a breath. Our lives are measured in seconds, not in years. By realizing this, we can better appreciate our lives.

✠ Those who cherish good fortune are those who do good things for others. Those who do good things for others always lead happy lives.

✠ Time passes swiftly indeed. Opportunities for learning slip through one's fingers only too easily. Grasp the chance now, or you will regret not having done so when you are old.

✠ A person will waste his time if he does nothing but groan about his troubles and pains. What makes the matter worse is that all his troubles and pains become twice as bad when he acts in such a manner.

※ To a wise person, time is a diamond, but to a fool, it is a lump of dirt. If we cherish our time as if it were a diamond and concentrate on doing good deeds, then nothing is impossible. However, if we waste our time heedlessly, we accomplish nothing and even become a burden to society.

※ Since we live in the world only for a few decades, the most important thing is our daily behavior. The success of our lives is the accumulation of all our daily actions. Our behavior each day determines whether our lives end up being meaningful or meaningless.

※ When a person becomes bogged down in the pursuit of wealth and forgets to use his wealth properly to help others, he is eventually abandoned by others. His life becomes more lonely and miserable than that of a poor person.

✠ The poor suffer materially and the rich suffer spiritually. The poor do everything they can to obtain things they want, while the rich are afraid of losing what they have. No wonder none of them can live in peace!

✠ Some of the poor are also poor mentally. These people are ignorant and narrow-minded. They are often eccentric and feel that they have been abandoned by others. They die without being noticed.

✠ Other people are materially poor but spiritually rich. Though destitute, they are warm and loving. They always smile and talk pleasantly. Their lives are happy and full.

29
The Place to Study
Buddhist Teachings
How to Get Along With Others

✖ If we want to accomplish something great, we must all work together. We must not feel prejudiced toward each other.

✖ When dealing with problems, we should act rationally and not purely on emotion. But when dealing with people, it is just the other way around: emotion is more important than rationality. In this way, we make ourselves popular and conduct our business efficiently.

✖ An upright heart is one of honesty and integrity, and it is the source of all our conduct. We must always be honest in our daily dealings with people. We should never deceive ourselves or others. We should always remember that an upright heart is the proper place to study Buddhist teachings. By maintaining this attitude, we become good disciples of Buddha and behave as he did.

�֎ When dealing with people, you should set a good example in the way you behave. You must purify your words, actions and thoughts, so that you may have respect for yourself and others.

✖ It is hard to be a loving person and it is hard to do good deeds. A person can become evil, greedy and corrupt just as soon as one bad thought crosses his mind. If we look closely, we will discover that because people seek wealth, fame and self-gratification, they have forgotten their basic, sacred nature.

Part 2
Questions and
Answers

Section 1: Human Affairs

Love

A Tzu Chi member who engaged in the fields of culture and education suffered the loss of her beloved husband. Master Cheng Yen consoled her. **"Don't count a man's life by his age, but by his achievements. Your husband made enormous contributions to his family and work. If you truly miss him, you should carry on his spirit of dedication and demonstrate your own talents as well. You should devote your time and energy to educating your children, purifying our society, and promoting our traditional virtues and culture.**

"Don't confine yourself only to your family," the Master continued, "and don't become depressed simply because you lost your husband's support. Chin up, chest out! Be confident! You should extend your love and concern to other people and do everything that you can do."

"I will try it gradually..." the member replied.

"Do it immediately," the Master interjected. "Life is filled with changes. We must seize the day. Someone asked me if I had any plans for the future. I said I certainly have plans and goals for the future, yet I must live for the moment. Our achievements in the future are based on our daily endeavors. The future is an accumulation of many 'todays.' You must do the best you can."

"I haven't been able to calm down during the last three months," the member confided. "I locked myself in my office, and didn't want to face others or go to any meetings. This situation continued until I dreamed that my husband told me that he would not be able to come back. Suddenly, Master, I understood what you meant by your words, 'You should stop missing him all the time.'"

"Your husband is physically free from all worldly worries," the Master explained. "Don't drag him down. It's your own problem if you can't let him go. Life is like a play, and each of us has a different role on the stage. Some play major roles, some minor roles. The major characters must continue to perform when the minor characters leave the stage. You have successfully played the different roles of wife, mother and good daughter-in-law. From now on, you have a new role to play — that of a bodhisattva. You must improve your knowledge and become a good teacher and helpful friend for your students. Teach all you know to your students and to others, without holding back. Education is filled with great enjoyment and unselfish giving. A true educator will teach people how to obtain spiritual happiness. We will never enjoy a fulfilling life if we are materially rich but spiritually poor. Promoting culture is aimed at purifying our hearts so that we can appreciate the significance of life and cherish our good fortune. People can then live happily and peacefully. That is why education is filled with great enjoyment. The education of people takes a hundred years to bear fruit. Be sure to devote your time and wisdom to your students and teach them all you know. That is what I call unselfish giving. Buddha's heart is filled with compassion, and a bodhisattva's heart is filled with great joy and the virtue of unselfish giving. What concerns a bodhisattva most is the plight of suffering creatures. You should do all you can to help others. The Heart Sutra says: 'You shall not worry. When there is no worry, there is no fear. You shall then avoid confusion and delusion.' Don't worry too much. Life is like a drama with a bodhisattva playing all sorts of roles on the stage. Hope that you can successfully and happily perform another role in a new play."

A member's husband always takes his troubles and frustrations home. What is worse, he likes to take them out on her. She is bothered by this constantly.

"A husband's psychological problems can only be healed by his wife," the Master told her. "Be sure to encourage him and show your love to him."

"I do," she replied. "Whenever he complains to me, I tell him to take it easy, because that's just the way things are."

"It is you who are wrong. Next time, you should tell him that you understand how bad he feels, that he has suffered much for you and your children, and that you really appreciate all his hard work."

Many people's complaints are related to family disputes. They wonder why love is filled with uncertainty.

Lovers always make a solemn pledge of everlasting love before they get married. However, their relationship sours once the honeymoon is over. It is silly of some people to commit suicide when they are deserted by their lovers. Do we only live in the pursuit of this kind of love? It is an evil act to destroy the body, which was given to us by our parents, simply because we are no longer loved by someone.

My wife had a heart attack because my son talked back rudely to her.

There are proper ways to educate our children. Be sure to encourage and praise them when they do things well, and remind them with just a few words when they behave badly. Timing is also very important when you want to correct their behavior. Times have changed. You should learn new methods of educating your children, just as your children learn new things every day.

Master, my husband doesn't want to take care of our family. I'm the one who has to look after the 17 people in our household. I can't take it any more.

His family is also your family. Your husband does so because he knows you are very capable. You are not tolerant enough if you regard the responsibility as suffering. It is true you have to look after 17 people. But remember that I must look after even more people. On the one hand, I must pray for hundreds of thousands of kind people, wishing their families good luck. I must assume the responsibility of educating the rich to the importance of planting the seeds of compassion and kindness in society. They can reap good fortune for themselves by performing kind and meritorious deeds for others. On the other hand, I also need to perform many charitable activities, such as the monthly relief for the poor program and raising funds for sudden emergencies. I, too, face many difficulties in dealing with so many people and projects. But I'm willing to do my work without complaint, despite the hardships and criticisms, so long as I can help all living beings.

A member complained: "I recently found out that while I was living abroad the past few years, my husband betrayed me by having an affair with one of my best friends. Now he's dead, but I'm still angry."

"You should not be angry with a person who has already passed away," the Master replied.

"I am not angry with the dead one," the member explained. "I am angry with the one that is still alive."

"You must not look back on things that have already happened," the Master responded. "Live only for today. We should live as if we were walking along a tightrope. You will fall if you keep looking back rather than forward. You should have forgiven him and shown love to the one he loved while he was still alive. What will you gain if you complain to others after he has gone?"

I'm worried about my son. He is 36 years old and still single.

Don't be pushy. You must let nature take its course. Otherwise, you might have regrets in the future.

If I make a resolution to do good things for others, will it help improve my son's karma?

It is our duty to do good things, and it will certainly bring good fortune to you if you make a resolution to do things that benefit others. We should bravely face the challenges that are destined to happen in our lives. Our karma, whether it is good or bad, can always serve as a warning to us. It is fixed according to our behavior. We should never ask for anything we do not deserve to have.

One member's husband was very obedient to her in many ways, but she was still unhappy. "Master," she said, "he is sometimes unfaithful. It really hurts. What should I do?"

Do not be too pushy. Love is like a ball: the harder you throw it against the ground, the higher it will bounce. Do not strangle your husband with excessive love. If you do so, he will politely keep you at arm's length. Be gentle and thoughtful to him, and not possessive. If you give him too much pressure, he will be obedient to you only in appearance. In fact, he is probably afraid of you in his heart. No wonder he commits acts of unfaithfulness. Try to extend your love to the one he loves. When he realizes what you are doing, he will feel grateful toward you. He will then cherish your love more deeply, realizing that you are providing space for him to grow and breathe. His heart is like a furnace: no matter how cold his heart may be, you can warm it with your sincere love.

Sad and angry parents came to see the Master and described how their son was killed in a dispute.

Reprisal breeds reprisal. You would do better by forgetting. Try to forgive those who killed your son. By doing so, you can create more good fortune for your son. You should also chant Buddha's name on behalf of your son, so that he can be freed from the bad karma. Do not grieve too much. You should understand that birth is the start of death and that death is the beginning of new life. Your son's death will help you understand the significance of life. Try to love other children who badly need your affection and concern. Your son will then be blessed.

My son is addicted to playing video games. I tell him not to waste his time on such things, but he always turns a deaf ear to me. This bothers me very much.

One can hardly control a man of 28. He will stop when he is tired of playing. As we often say, "He will be bored with the game when it is out of fashion." Do not nag him. Simply remind him now and then.

Every family has some sort of problem.

Since you know that, you should always let go of your worries and remain calm.

How can a professional woman take care of her family and career at the same time?

One of the best things for a woman to have is the glory of the maternal instinct. It is good for a professional woman to get ahead in her career, but she should not extinguish the glory of her maternal instinct.

I know it is against Buddha's teachings to hate others. Even so, I can't help but hate my husband because he is having an affair.

It is so difficult for the ordinary person to distinguish between true love and infatuation. You should love the one your husband loves. Try to change your common love into a bodhisattva's pure love. Religious faith is more than only taking part in religious rituals. You must understand the Earth Treasury Bodhisattva's great spirit of compassion, instead of only chanting his name all the time. Your husband and mother-in-law are just the right persons for you to show your love and concern to.

A certain Tzu Chi member was very much concerned about his children's marriages, a situation upon which the Master expounded.

Parents give physical birth to their children, but they cannot give them a spiritual life or good fortune. Each person has his own fate. If we are determined to walk on the Path of the Bodhisattvas, we must make a strong commitment to extend our love to all living beings for the rest of our lives. All parents should acknowledge the fact that they bear responsibility for their children, but do not exercise rights over them.

My husband is having an affair. How can I cope with the pain?

Don't call it an affair. You should view it as fate. It is part of your karma. You should accept it bravely. You should keep loving and thanking your husband. He has given you a chance to see that our lives are filled with changes. You can grasp this chance to examine your conscience and readjust yourself. Do not see it as a form of pain. It is a sin if you commit suicide, since you destroy the body given you by your beloved parents. How can you eliminate your bad karma if you do not have a body to do good deeds? Both husband and wife should feel grateful if their marriage is pleasant. They should remain calm if their marriage is not as wonderful as they expected.

All my children are adults now, but I still doubt that they can take care of themselves. It troubles me.

You must let go. Your extreme concern for your children will cause you nothing but headaches. Your children can take care of themselves because they have grown up. Our lives are filled with changes and uncertainty. You should grasp every chance to do good deeds.

How can a housewife become a good Buddhist?

You are a human being, not an animal. As a human being, you should abide by the rules of society. Only when a housewife fulfills a housewife's duty will she qualify to become a Buddhist. A good housewife's contributions to her family and society are enormous. In fact, she has three different roles to play in order to become a good Buddhist.

First, she must be a good daughter-in-law. She needs to embrace the concept of filial piety by serving her father- and mother-in-law well. It is always wiser to respect the two living buddhas at home than to worship a stone buddha in a temple. Second, she must be a good wife. She should look after her husband and help society sweep away pornography. She should also encourage her husband to devote his efforts to his work and his faith. Third, she must be a good mother. She should increase her knowledge in every field, so that she can become a good teacher and guide for her children. She should make sure that her children are healthy and strong, both physically and mentally.

My family is wealthy. However, my only son treats me as if I were his enemy.

Karma is created in one's previous lives. You can do nothing but face it when it comes. Try to be nice to him and wish him good luck. When we die, we can take nothing with us but our karma, no matter if it is good or bad. There are many examples to demonstrate that the wealth of a family does not bring happiness to its children. In fact, wealth sometimes creates a lot of headaches. Wealth can mean good luck or bad luck for a person. It all depends on the way you use it.

I feel that we should begin to improve the educational environment in our families, but I don't know how.

You don't need to hold any special activity. Just try to encourage all parents to love all children, not just their own. If you keep inflating the same balloon, it will explode before long. You should use a mother's heart to love all living beings, but use a bodhisattva's wisdom to educate your own children.

I know that the one I love lied to me once, but I still love him. Whenever I see him, I feel like I want to punch him in the nose. But when he is away, I miss him dearly. I even want to die.

Do not be so silly as to want to die for someone else. It is so easy to die. You should make your existence valuable. You can do a lot of great things for others. So why don't you? Our lives are short. That you have been mistreated by someone is not so bad. What is really bad is when you don't make the most of your life.

My daughter's fiance is inferior to her in education and social status.

We should not be overly concerned about a person's status. Nor should we measure a person's wisdom by his diploma. Virtue is what really counts. We should plan to get married because of love, not because of social status or other such attractions.

Many parents pressure their children to excel in their schoolwork.

The love between mother and child is great. However, it will disturb your child if he knows your concern is based on his performance in school. You should instead calm your worries by chanting Buddha's sutras. We are always gaining something and losing something. Besides, anyone can become a master in his field.

My husband scolded my son by saying that he would not make a success of himself until the sky and earth changed.

The scolding was actually a blessing. The sky and earth are changing all the time. Sometimes it is hot and sunny, and other times it becomes cold and cloudy. Your son will be very successful. Try to be understanding, for doing so will make you luckier and wiser.

Mothers-in-Law

A young woman who always talks back rudely when being scolded by her mother-in-law went to see the Master in Hualien.

"Your behavior was wrong," the Master said to her. "When your mother-in-law scolds you, you should not talk back."

This woman went home and did as the Master had said. Later, she met the Master again. "I did exactly what you taught me, but my mother-in-law became even more furious. She said I was turning a deaf ear to her. What should I do now?"

"How did you respond when she scolded you?" the Master asked. "I just kept silent and turned a deaf ear to her," the woman replied.

"Again, you were wrong," the Master told her. "When she is furious, you should behave obediently. When you throw a ball against the ground, it will bounce back, but when you throw a ball against a sponge, it does not bounce back. When she scolds you the next time, just smile to her and say, 'Yes, Mother, I understand and I will correct my faults.' If she is still mad at you, you should keep smiling and endure her angry words."

Later, the woman spoke with the Master again. "It worked," she said. "I kept on smiling at her while she was scolding me. Finally, she started laughing along with me when she saw my smiling face. Now my mother-in-law doesn't scold me anymore. She encourages me to listen to sutras, and she even helps me do the dishes."

When my mother-in-law passed away, we were all living abroad together. Nothing I arranged for in the funeral parlor was in accordance with Chinese custom. Ever since then, I have been fighting with my brother- and sister-in-law, because they feel I was disrespectful to their mother.

Let bygones be bygones. If you continue to argue, your mother-in-law will not be able to rest in peace.

A wealthy, elderly woman said: "Master, I don't want to give my money to my daughter-in-law for fear that she might misuse it. She is angry with me over this, even though I feel my intentions are good."

"Why don't you do as she wishes, since your intention is to help her? You should give your money to your daughter-in-law so that she can learn how to manage money. You will be free from the burden of controlling your money and will win her gratitude. You are healthy now, but will you be able to manage your money when you get sick? You had better put your daughter-in-law in charge of the family fortune. She will feel grateful to you and will treat you nicer."

The woman met the Master a month later. "Thank you so much, Master. My life has become more enjoyable. First of all, I don't have to worry about the family finances. Secondly, my daughter-in-law gives me NT$20,000 [about US$800] per month. There is enough left over for me to donate to charity. The interesting thing is that in the past I did not dare donate that much money because I was afraid of exceeding the family budget."

Illness

A terminal liver cancer patient became a disciple of the Master.

A man's life can be divided in two. There is the profane, mortal life, and the pure, eternal life of wisdom. A man should always be prepared to discard the profane one when it becomes old and unable to be fixed, like a shabby house. We should grasp every chance to learn Buddha's teachings. We should also make the most of our limited lives to cultivate a bodhisattva's kind heart. Do not forget that when the time comes for us to abandon this short, painful life, we still possess an eternal life of wisdom.

Physical illness is not to be feared. What is really to be feared is when a man becomes ill spiritually. Cheer up and wipe that frown off your face. Life is short. We should live happily. Illness is not horrible. A person simply needs to live at ease with it.

It is proper for you to accept Buddhism. But you must heed my advice — stop worrying about life and death! A lot of patients become neurotic after finding out what illness they have. They go to see different doctors and take all sorts of medicine, only making matters worse. Yet when they decide to let go of all the treatments, they feel immeasurably better. Do not put pressure on yourself. Let nature take its course.

I understand Buddha's teachings, and I have been trying to act like Buddha for years. But now I am sick. I feel fearful and don't know how to cope with it. What must I do to obtain the blessings of Buddha?

We do not receive the blessings of Buddha simply by trying to imitate his behavior. As Buddhists, our aim is to cultivate courage. Buddha said that karma is irreversible. The true essence of acting like Buddha lies in accepting our karma fearlessly and calmly.

"Life is but a meaningless trip," exclaimed an elderly secular Buddhist devotee [one who cultivates morality in the daily world] who chanted sutras and worshipped Buddha every day, even though he could not see clearly due to diabetes.

This is not true. Your life's journey will not be a waste, because you have learned Buddha's teachings and wisdom.

Another elderly secular Buddhist devotee who was also of declining health said he believed his days were numbered. He hoped he would have a stronger body when he was reincarnated so that he could help more people. But what bothered him was that he felt he might not become a Buddhist in his next life.

Let nature take its course. You will be able to help many people if you can recover from your illness sooner. The people living around us, no matter how many of them there are, need our care and concern very much. If we cannot help deliver them from their troubles now, how can we expect to help them in the next life? No one can act like Buddha when he is out of touch with living beings. We should always try to maintain good relationships with all creatures while we ourselves are still alive. Do not treat yourself as a sick man. Try to relax and live actively, for time is precious. Your strong desire to live is important.

Master, be sure to take good care of yourself.

No one is perfect. Each of us has some physical or mental problems. One should not be afraid of physical illness. It is only part of our bad karma. I have suffered from various illnesses. However, my heart is at peace. What really worries me are the obstacles lying ahead of me regarding the four missions of the Tzu Chi Association. I would rather replace those obstacles with my own physical pains. The world is full of tolerance. We must have the spirit of tolerance while living in the world. Our bodies are only external forms. I hope you can pay more attention to my life of wisdom.

A medical student expressed deep sorrow over the death of one of his close relatives.

The Master consoled him. "Since you are a medical student, you will deal with many patients in the future. You should have a deep understanding of life and death. In Buddhism, death is a form of rebirth. The dead leave for a new life. Life and death are cyclical. Therefore, death is not sad. We should pray for the dead and chant sutras for them."

"What can I do for the dead?" the medical student continued.

"Be a good student. Study hard so that you can save a lot of people in the future. Our bodies are given to us by our parents. The best way you can show your gratitude to them is to be a good doctor."

What is your opinion of life?

Our lives are not worth mentioning. However, a person's life of wisdom is truly valuable and can last forever. Also, it can be an example for our offspring to follow.

An elderly gentleman was suffering from stomach cancer.

Thirty percent of a person's illness is physical pain, while the remaining seventy percent is mental pain. A sick person needs to maintain a tranquil mind. You need to release your anguish aloud, whether the sounds are groans of pain or joyous sutra chants. You must demonstrate your sorrow or happiness with facial expressions. You should be aware that your joyful sounds and happy facial expressions will bring comfort to others as well as yourself.

I have been suffering from chest pain for years. I feel I only have a short time left, and my desire to live is growing weaker and weaker.

You should rise and sleep according to a set schedule. Have a physical checkup or see a doctor when necessary. Do not lose the strong will to struggle. You should let doctors take care of your body, but let bodhisattvas look after your mind and soul.

One's Mindset

A guest came to see the Master. "After reading the first volume of *Still Thoughts*, I realize that you have a whole set of philosophical principles. Asia Weekly magazine depicted you as a 'mountain climber.' May I ask you to describe any changes in your mindset that occurred when you went 'mountain climbing' over the last ten years?"

"Each of us has his own goal in life. Before setting that goal, we should consider it carefully and then make a good choice. After setting the goal, we should march toward it resolutely. I want to give you a good explanation by using an analogy. There are two routes by which one can go from the Abode of Still Thoughts to the Tzu Chi Hospital, the main road or the country road. I can go to the hospital on either one. However, I often go on the small country road. The reason is simple: I enjoy looking at the beautiful scenery along that road.

"I have experienced all sorts of obstacles in my work over the decades. I have always regarded those troubles as scenery along the road, and I have tried to deal with them with a calm attitude.

"When we go mountain climbing, our eventual goal is to climb to the top of the mountain. We should not let the scenery along our way cause us to stray from our goal."

The guest then asked, "If a person likes to help the poor and appreciate the beautiful scenery along the road at the same time, will these two contradict each other?"

"They won't if you feel at ease. It depends on your mindset."

"Were you inspired by things or people that you experienced before you became a nun?"

"I hardly have time to look backward or forward. I only live for today."

"The missions of the Tzu Chi Association will be carried on forever," the guest observed. "How can we keep them operating smoothly?"

"Buddha taught us the concept that a good cause results in a good effect. What happens to you now can be attributed to things you did in the past, and what you will achieve in the future is based on what you do at this very moment. Thus, do not daydream about the future. You should work hard right now. Take the Tzu Chi Hospital and the Still Thoughts Hall as two examples. We completed these two big construction projects through enormous determination and hard work."

Why do living beings have to suffer so much pain?

You suffer a lot of pain if you do not have a clear understanding of life. However, you will be very much at ease if you possess a clear understanding. The Buddha said that everyone is born equal, and each of us has some buddha-nature. You can become as good as the Buddha if you are willing to improve yourself constantly. In order to become a buddha, you must walk on the Path of the Bodhisattvas. You must study the Buddha's teachings and help all living creatures to attain enlightenment. Then joy and suffering will be all the same to you.

How should I get rid of my stubborn attachments to things?

There are two ways to eliminate one's egotism. First, you should try to shrink yourself to become as small as a human cell. Second, you should try to expand yourself to become as big as the universe. You will then be able to accommodate all sorts of people and things. It is easy to say this, but it is extremely difficult to put this into practice. As we often say: we should strengthen our will power by dealing with all sorts of problems.

A member asked the Master to help him cultivate wisdom.

A person will never be able to cultivate wisdom if he is heartless and cruel. You should try to eliminate all the unnecessary worries from your mind, for they will overshadow the bright side of your heart. How can you maintain a reasonable and wise mind under that condition?

A member who happened to be sitting face-to-face with the Master in a meeting felt shy and grabbed a book to look at as a way to shield her face. By coincidence, a picture of the Buddha was printed on the book cover.

I hope you always exhibit a face like Buddha's when you cover up your ordinary face.

I want to thank you for helping me get rid of my superstitious beliefs. Now my family is doing fine and my husband's career is going very well.

If we intend to change the bad habits of others, we should first change our own. Each of us has a different character, just as we have different faces. We often say that it is easier to move a mountain than to change a man's character. Actually, we do not need to change our character, since it also contains our buddha-nature. Imagine what we would be if we removed our buddha-nature from our characters. What we should really remove is our bad habits.

Do paradise and hell really exist?

You are living in paradise when you behave kindly toward others, but you are living in hell when you behave maliciously.

How should I maintain a healthy mind?

Most people's minds are like a dirt-covered mirror. You should constantly wipe your mind clean with Buddha's teachings.

"Master, I am sick all over," a member said. "However, the doctor said I was all right. But you see I'm really too sick to work and..."

The Master interrupted to say, "Oh, you are truly sick, and it is too serious to be cured."

"I am?" the startled member said.

"Yes you are. You are indeed sick mentally. No one can cure your mental illness except yourself. But a mental illness will turn into a physical one if you do not take action to stop it. If you wait too long, your illness will truly be hopeless."

What are the most beautiful and least beautiful things in the world?

A loving heart is the most beautiful thing, while a lustful thought is the least beautiful thing in the world.

"I am very absent-minded," a guest said. "Whenever I try to do one thing, my mind strays to something else. How can I learn to concentrate?"

"You can concentrate your mind by knowing how to use time properly and how to seize the day," the Master answered. "Be sure to focus your attention on the work you are doing now. Be ready to do a good job when any chance comes, just as the fabled roc was always ready to fly high into the sky when a strong wind blew. Mindfulness is natural, not something you can do on purpose."

The guest continued. "Since mindfulness is natural, why do I need to work hard at concentrating my mind? Isn't this contradictory?"

"When you become used to concentrating, you do not need to pay attention to whether or not you are concentrating. You can walk or eat easily. Do you need to concentrate when you do these?"

"That sounds very reasonable," the guest said. "However, it is easier to understand this sort of reasoning than to actually put it into practice."

"It is not difficult when you truly understand it. It is difficult only when you assume it is difficult."

Why is our society in turmoil? Whenever something unexpected happens, people become anxious and fearful.

This is so because there is a lack of conscience and fair judgment in our society. People tend to act inappropriately when they are filled with biased judgments.

A secular Buddhist devotee spoke about geomancy.

We Buddhists are concerned only about people's minds, not about geomancy.

Life

One member asked about the concept of life.

You must be responsible for every word you say. Be aware of the goal you are planning at the present time, but do not let worries over things that might happen tomorrow deter you from pursuing your goal in life. We should plan for the future, yet be attentive to what we are engaged in right now.

Master, your memory is getting bad because you are too busy and take care of too many things.

A man's physical body and memory will become poorer and poorer as he gets older, even if he has been lazy all his life and accomplished nothing. Age, not hard work, slows the functions of our bodies. That is why we should seize the day.

What is a fulfilling life?

To have a fulfilling life, we should respect our superiors and love our subordinates. I believe other people will respect us if we treat them with love and courtesy. It is a fulfilling life if we respect and love one another.

How can I help myself and other people as well?

You can help yourself by eliminating your faults, and you can help others by leading them to correct their own faults.

Tolerating Insults

Someone asked the Master to talk about the importance of tolerance and patience.

Of the six virtues, tolerance is the most important. Friction between people is caused by a lack of tolerance and patience. A person can never, cultivate the other five virtues — unselfish giving, abiding by the Buddhist disciplines, self-improvement, meditation, and wisdom — without having cultivated tolerance. You need to be tolerant and patient in order to do things that benefit all living creatures. Each living creature has a different nature. If we want to help people change their bad habits, we need to wait patiently for the right moment. We can then accomplish our task as easily as skimming oil off the surface of a pool of water. When a person is tolerant and patient, he is able to deal with people smoothly and reasonably. Thus, he can promote the six virtues without expending too much effort.

Master, I want to be your good disciple. However, the more I tolerate a certain person's insults, the more he tries to take advantage of me. I am just about to explode. What should I do?

Try to regard that person as Buddha, who arranges various types of distress just to test you. How could you be angry with Buddha, since you want to imitate his behavior?

How can a person get along well with others?

When you want to talk to others about their faults, don't yell at them with sharp words, but speak nicely. By doing so, you avoid the risk of being hated by them. We should tolerate bad people, but at the same time we must be careful of them.

What kind of people can you not forgive?

I can forgive anyone who is rude to me except those who lie. To err is human, but to be dishonest is unpardonable.

Compassion

An 80-year-old gentleman spoke to the Master. "My grandson said I look younger than before. Is this possible?"

It is because your heart is filled with love. A loving heart is a beautiful heart that not only breeds happiness among the people around you, but also purifies your body and mind as well as their bodies and minds.

Some members of the Tzu Chi Association often pray to Buddha and his disciples for blessings and good fortune for all the people of the world.

Besides praying to them, you should also perform good deeds, abide by human ethics, respect the old and love small children in order to fulfill your wishes. Otherwise, how can you obtain good fortune?

"Master, why do we feel so happy whenever we meet you?" a perplexed member asked. "And Master, why does my own son always talk back to me so rudely?"

The Master replied, "These situations are because the karmic relationship between you and me will be continued for many lives, whereas the karma between you and your son is limited to this life only."

"If the relationship between you and me will be continued for many lives," the member continued, "then why am I only a secular disciple of yours?"

"It is because you have too many worldly desires."

What is compassion?

Compassion requires us to love those with whom we do not have a special relationship and to share in the unhappiness of others. Compassion is concerned with all living creatures.

Today's young people like to drive fast.

Driving fast does not mean you are a good driver, whereas driving slowly shows that you are a polite gentleman. Besides, you should drive slowly in order to protect the bodhisattva in your heart.

Many people wonder how they can eliminate worries and troubles.

You need to better understand Buddhist teachings, reduce worldly desires, and extend your love to all living beings in order to eliminate worry.

Is it impolite to read your books while lying in bed?

Politeness is not demonstrated by small mannerisms. True politeness is when you take my words seriously and put them into practice in your daily conduct.

How do you define real love?

Wisdom is the prerequisite for a pure love that is without self-consideration and desire. I define real love as "great kindness even to strangers and great compassion for all." We must offer our pure love even to people with whom we do not have a special relationship, and we must share compassionately in the unhappiness of others.

Daily Affairs

I was wondering if I should take my children to visit impoverished families.

That's fine. Take them as if it were a picnic. You will be showing them what we Tzu Chi people are doing. Besides, it will be a good opportunity to teach them about gratitude. Many children realize how lucky and wealthy they are after visiting poor families. They will better appreciate what they have. But you must remind your children of one very important thing: be gentle to the poor. Complaining about the filthy living conditions of the poor is forbidden.

Tzu Chi people seem to be rich.

They are not only well off financially, but also rich in love, wisdom and compassion!

"Tzu Chi has grown so large now," a member noted. "What will we do when you are gone?"

The Master was silent for a moment, before responding in a sentimental tone. "Why do people always worry about death? Why don't they simply seize the day and do what they must."

We donated a lot of money to build the Tzu Chi Hospital in Hualien. However, some of us cannot use the facility very easily because it is located too far away.

Out of the eight ways to create good fortune, helping patients care for their illnesses is the most important one. The reason we set up the hospital in eastern Taiwan was because that part of the island lacked medical facilities. A Buddhist should strive to be a big-hearted person. Realize that any hospital is constructed to serve the needs of sick people. Isn't it wonderful that you don't need it?

Thank you so much for reeducating my wife. She has become more gentle, diligent and thoughtful since she became a member of the Tzu Chi Association.

It was not I who reeducated your wife and other members. After joining the association, many people have experienced the unhappy side of life, such as witnessing illness or death. They now realize that life is filled with changes. These experiences constantly remind them of how short life is and how important it is to correct their wrong behavior. We can often learn from interacting with a group of people. I really appreciate the support of our members' spouses. They have been a big help to me.

The Master's commitment is great, but what should we disciples do to help realize it?

A centipede has a hundred legs that are well coordinated with one another. We must be of one mind and concert our efforts. Then, we will certainly realize our goals.

What should we do to introduce Buddhism to others?

Buddha introduced his religion to the world for the sake of saving living beings. Buddha has to serve all living beings first in order to let them understand Buddhism. Therefore, we Tzu Chi members first engage in our four Tzu Chi missions in order to do good deeds for all living beings. We can then introduce them to Buddhism.

What should we do when a poor patient stays in Tzu Chi Hospital for a long time without paying the bill?

I keep telling the doctors at the hospital that it is their job to look after the poor patients and my job to take care of the bills. Poor patients can go to the Social Welfare Department at the hospital. They can enjoy either a discount or completely free diagnosis and treatment if they meet our criteria. Also, we should encourage patients to stand on their own feet after they leave the hospital. They can pay for bills in installments after they find work.

Master, I am so moved by the things accomplished by Tzu Chi. I wish I could help more, but I am in poor health.

The fact that our health becomes poor is why we must realize we do not have time to waste. Our body is a vehicle for carrying out our religious faith. We can do good deeds if we sincerely want to.

You have instituted a rule that all donations must be used for Tzu Chi's charitable activities, while you and others who live in the Abode of Still Thoughts rely only on what you produce. Was this a decision you made when you first became a nun? If so, why?

Even before I became a nun, I always made it a rule for myself to make my own living. I still live by that rule. To stand on my own feet is one of two principles I pursue. The other is unselfish giving. Our association's accomplishments can be attributed to the unselfish giving of each member. After establishing the Tzu Chi Association, I was careful to separate association funds, donated by the public, from administration funds, which we ourselves earn. What our association has achieved today is based on the members' sincerity and honesty. We should never allow any careless mistake or character flaw to tarnish the association's good reputation.

What is the most profound significance of the four missions [charity, medicine, education and culture] of the Tzu Chi Association?

The most profound significance of the missions is that we put our principles into action. The missions of charity and medicine concern our actions, and the missions of education and culture concern our principles. The future development of Tzu Chi will be meaningful only if our actions and principles go together. If we have the best philosophical principles in the world but do not put them into practice, then it is only empty talk. If we try to do great things but do them for the wrong reasons, then we will accomplish nothing.

Buddha says, "Less desire, more contentment," yet Tzu Chi has more and more projects. Isn't it against Buddha's teachings to have many desires?

There are two different types of desire. The first kind involves following the saints. The second kind is the desire for evil pleasures, such as wealth, wanton sex, fame, lavish food and idle sleeping.

Master, I tried to introduce Tzu Chi to a rich man in the hope that he would join us and do good things. He said he wasn't interested and turned me down.

The work of Tzu Chi needs to be done by people who are willing to volunteer their time and resources. We should introduce our work to everyone, whether rich or poor. We should let them know that our association is a good place to make meritorious contributions. We can congratulate those who are willing to join us, but we should not express disappointment toward those who are unwilling.

Learning

How can we learn from Buddha's wisdom in order to avoid becoming attached to things?

You should not become attached to things, since you know this is wrong. People are so smart: they make so many distinctions between things and thus they have so many contradictions. That is why they fail to perceive the simplicity of human affairs and have so many attachments.

I have been busy soliciting donations everywhere. Therefore, I have not had that much time to read sutras.

Daily life is a form of living sutra. It not only increases our wisdom, but also trains us to maintain our tranquillity. Buddha's teachings cannot be sought in black and white on paper. By dealing with people every day, we learn not to be influenced by external events, and from this we develop our wisdom. On the Path of the Bodhisattvas, we can cultivate good fortune for ourselves and other people. This is what the sutras teach us: good fortune and wisdom go together.

What is the proper way to learn?

You need to read carefully, listen carefully, think carefully, and skillfully apply what you have learned when you deal with problems or people.

Doing Work

Master, why are you always reminding us to make good use of every second?

Life is uncertain, and our lives depend on the air we breathe. Life would cease if we could not breathe. That is why we need to make good use of each second.

Have you come to any conclusion regarding what you have accomplished over the last 25 years?

My conclusion is that I did just what I should have done. My mind would be in a state of confusion if I kept looking back on what I did, and I would be in a state of delusion if I kept dreaming about the future. On the other hand, I certainly must continue to seize this day, marching toward my goals in accordance with my blueprint.

Master, do you have any plans for the future?

I have some plans, but it is important for me to seize the day. I must make good use of my 86,400 seconds each day.

I have often done many good things for others. So why is it that my business is still not doing well and I'm not making any progress in my moral cultivation?

You need to make the proper choices in doing good things. Buddha's sutras talk about the Ten Devils, such as the devil of good deeds and the devil of confidence. You could be easily fooled by the devil of good deeds if you did not make wise choices in the deeds you choose to do. Don't keep telling yourself that your business will be great simply because you have done so much for the poor. If you do, you will bring worry to yourself each time you do good things for others. That is why we describe people such as you as being fooled by the devil of good deeds. You cannot make progress in your moral cultivation this way.

One Tzu Chi member became smug and self-satisfied after receiving high praise from other members for his outstanding contribution to the group.

He is not praiseworthy. Who is more praiseworthy — the man who is capable of carrying a burden that weighs 10 kilos yet carries only eight, or the man who is only capable of carrying one kilo but strains as best he can to carry one and one-half kilos?

It is difficult to ask others to join in one's work. However, we often need the help of others in order to complete our tasks. How can we motivate others to join us and work together joyfully?

If you want to gain something, you must first give unselfishly to others. You will never gain what you want if you are too demanding. The reason life may seem tough is because you may be demanding something you do not deserve to have.

Some people call you Taiwan's "Mother Teresa" or its "Albert Schweitzer," or a great bodhisattva that came into the world to fulfill her commitment to save people. What do you think?

I just do what I should do.

Master, how do you control your subordinates?

It is very hard to control other people. People, in fact, do not like to be controlled by someone else. The best method of personnel management is to let people develop a good mindset of self-discipline.

It is very hard to get along with people. It is so easy to offend them.

The reason you cannot get along with others smoothly is because you sometimes talk too much when you should keep silent, and you sometimes keep your mouth closed tight when you should be giving your opinion.

Can we refuse to do a job when we feel it is beyond our capabilities?

A real gentleman will try everything he can to improve himself, despite any hardship or difficulty. Nothing is impossible if we work diligently. There is a Chinese saying that goes, "A gentleman will never abandon a chance to do something good for others." How, then, can you refuse to do a job that will benefit others?

I have trouble controlling my bad temper. What should I do?

A bad temper will not only bother yourself, but also make you a nuisance to others. A good temper will not only bring you happiness, but make you more popular. Your personality and sense of morality depend on whether you have a good or bad temper. If you have a bad temper, it will ruin your character, even though you may otherwise be a kind person.

Worries

I work in a beauty parlor. The busier I am, the more meaningless I feel life is.

You probably lack quality in your life. That is why you feel life is meaningless. You can fill your life with Buddha's teachings. You can listen to taped sutras while serving your customers. In doing so, you will not only be cleaning hair, but also purifying hearts. You should set a goal for your life.

A hospital nurse was often irritated about having to work in the operating room with a famous but bad-tempered doctor.

Try to deal with the doctor with a sense of humor. Let him vent his resentment and then comfort him with gentle words. I believe his mind will gradually become peaceful.

A Tzu Chi member came to the Master. "I have been read-ing sutras daily and I also understand the importance of cultivating one's morality. But why do I still have so many worries?"

"I can help those who do not understand Buddha's teachings," the Master responded. "But since you know Buddha's teachings and the sutras and still cannot find peace and relaxation, there is nothing I can do for you."

The member continued, "I am never able to let worries just slide off my shoulder."

"It is beyond Buddha's ability to help you if you keep thinking this way. You should correct your mindset since you already know it is wrong. Don't let things bother you."

"My career is pretty successful," a businessman reflected. "I own everything I want. But why do I still feel life is meaningless?"

Ordinary people focus too much attention on them-selves. They tend to become greedy and too ambitious. When they have earned 10 million dollars, they want to earn 30 million. They are never content with what they have. Buddha said, "Stability is the greatest fortune, and contentment is the greatest wealth." You will be happier if you share the fruits of what you have harvested with others. Do not forget that you are a member of society. You cannot accomplish anything great without the support of other people. Besides, you cannot take any material things with you when you go to meet Buddha.

Desires

Master, were you born with your perseverance, courage and confidence? Or, were you forced to acquire these?

A person's strength will be boundless when he does not desire something he does not deserve to have. Preoccupation with trivia saps one's spirit, perseverance and courage.

A guest at the Abode of Still Thoughts praised the Master. "I learned a lot about your achievements even before I came to see you in Hualien. I am very happy to see you today. I have been exposed to various religions since I was 20 years old, but I never felt like I belonged to any particular one. Fortunately, I have read your books and am inspired by your wise words. Also, I am deeply impressed by your sense of tolerance and your spirit of perseverance. You have successfully freed yourself from

both the bondage of secular rules and the restrictions of religion. Consequently, more people have come to participate in your charitable activities. The gap between people has been largely eliminated. This, to me, is the most important of the great things you have achieved."

"I only let nature take its course," the Master responded. "I do not tolerate people deliberately."

"This is what touched my heart the most," the guest continued. "Your manner is so natural and humble when you talk about things you have been doing."

"It is natural for fish to live in water and humans to breathe air. To tolerate others is also part of the natural order. Being members of society, we should care about and accept one another naturally. People nowadays behave in unnatural ways. That is why they regard natural things as abnormal."

Social Customs

"Our social customs are no longer good," an attorney observed. "It is painful to see a group of relatives sue one another for money."

From a religious person's perspective, I feel the fewer court trials the better. The fewer trials we engage in, the more time we will have to do good deeds. It is painful to go through a legal process, whether you win or lose.

A secular Buddhist disciple asked for the Master's opinion about investing in the stock market.

It's a good thing when you increase a society's circulation of capital and property by buying and selling stocks. But when you speculate on the stock exchange in an opportunistic way, you not only make others suffer from the ups and downs of prices, but also make yourself lazy and greedy. Judging from the Buddhist concept of cause and effect, I think of speculators as real trouble-makers, even though they might not intentionally mean to bring ruin to other people or their own families.

How can we resolve confrontations between labor and management?

In the past, people worked to live. They were worried about being fired by their boss. The tables are turning now: the bosses are worried about losing their careers. In order to be a good manager, you should get rid of the "I'm the boss, you're the employee" mentality.

How can I distinguish between complexity and simplicity?

Simplicity can be very complex, and complexity can be very simple. Eating is a simple task, but you can choke to death if you eat carelessly.

What are the responsibilities of Tzu Chi members?

There are two things that need to be done by Tzu Chi commissioners and members: help the poor and educate the rich. Not all rich people are loving people. Buddha said that each of us has a loving heart. People, however, have become habitually selfish. They tend to do whatever they can to earn a lot of money, but it is hard to say whether they will be willing to share their gains with others. Some people lose what they achieve and must be supported by other people's contributions. Individuals and society are closely linked. One will never share the results of one's successes with others if one is selfish. Imagine what our society would be like if everyone was selfish. It is the Tzu Chi commissioners' duty to educate the rich and to reveal the love in their hearts. Fine grains of sand accumulate to make a pagoda. If we could accumulate rich people's contributions, it would swell into such a great power.

Questions and Answers

Answers

Section 2: Religion

Cause and Effect

I have never done anything bad as an adult. But I have encountered a series of unlucky incidents recently. I am quite puzzled and nervous. I plan to seek the help of a fortune-teller.

It is our duty to act properly. Most people in the world do nothing bad in their lives. However, they seldom do anything good, either. It is nothing special if you never do anything bad to others, but it is important to do things that benefit others in order to change your karma and fate. It is useless to have good intentions yet never put them into practice.

Why do some people live a comfortable life even though they have never done anything good?

In order to answer your question, we need to discuss the karma from one's previous three lives. We often meet two groups of people: those who are kind and nice toward others, and those who are bossy and cruel. However, people of the former group sometimes have rougher lives than the latter. Why? It is because of the karma determined in their previous lives. Although karma is something we cannot change, we can be completely at ease if we face it calmly and take Buddha's teachings as our spiritual support.

I have never seen "cause." What is it?

Cause is like a seed. If I told you the seed was a tree, you would not believe me because it could only be viewed as a seed from any perspective. This is what we mean when we say "a cause without the proper conditions." But when the seed is in the ground and receives water and sunlight, it will grow, bloom and eventually bear fruit. A kind heart of unselfish giving is like a seed. You should seize the right opportunity to plant the seed so that it can grow into a big tree. And you should wait patiently for the results. Do not think you are going to reap the fruit the very next day after you plant the seed. You might ruin the seed completely if you dig it up to see whether it is still alive. Greedy people only want to save the rice harvested two years ago for use in the future. They keep saving and accumulating rice until it is all eaten up by worms. Don't forget that only the unhulled rice harvested this year can be used as seeds. If we intend to do something, we should do it immediately, and we should not be greedy.

I have always behaved properly in my life. Even so, why don't things always turn out the way I wish?

You are doing pretty well now. However, the good effect has not shown up yet. All the unpleasant matters you are facing now can be attributed to the unfavorable cause made in the past. Cause is a seed.

Eliminating Disaster

Master, when is your birthday?

Each new day to me is like a birthday. The moment I open my eyes in the morning is a new beginning for me.

How can I eliminate misfortune and increase my good fortune?

It all depends on you. You must cultivate virtue in order to eliminate disaster. You can avoid confronting others by giving in a little. You can change a potential disaster into an incident of good fortune by showing a gentle, loving attitude.

People often ask the Master how they can increase their good fortune.

You can increase the abundance of good fortune for yourself by doing things that benefit others.

Superstition

Can we eliminate bad karma by chanting sutras?

The principle of cause and effect would be violated if we eliminated bad karma by chanting sutras. Being human, we will all die someday. You must get off the bus at the stop that corresponds with the mileage you paid for when you bought your ticket. You should do things beneficial to others prior to any arrival of bad karma.

When we face a problem, should we use fortune-tellers or pray to the gods for help?

Face reality bravely and resolutely. We should remain joyful, even when under the challenge of distress. You can get yourself into big trouble by blindly seeking help from gods or fortune-tellers, because they might confuse you or mislead you into making a wrong decision.

I have suffered from an undetermined illness since I had a car accident. I'm very confused and uneasy because I can't figure out what's going on. I often pray to the gods in any temple or church I come across.

You should not believe in any religion you hear about. Make a well thought-out decision. Choose an orthodox religion. There is an educational function in any religion. Churches and temples should be places for learning about human affairs. You must relax first, and then you will be able to calm down. The so-called demons will leave you alone when you are in a quiet state of peacefulness. They exist nowhere but in your heart. We Buddhists believe in the concept of unavoidable karma. Whether we like it or not, our fate is destined to happen, no matter what. Try to accept any unfortunate episodes along the way with a joyful attitude, because they will soon pass.

Faith

I don't think I have enough insight to perceive the wisdom recorded in the Buddhist sutras. What should I do?

You should chant the sutras until your heart becomes like the Buddha's. You will then become as wise as the Buddha. The Buddha's heart is filled with great compassion.

Someone suggested that I prostrate myself before the Earth Treasury Sutra.

The Earth Treasury Bodhisattva vowed that he would not attain enlightenment until all the souls in hell had been saved. It would be better if you made a vow that was as noble as the one he made than if you prostrated yourself before the sutra written by him. You should worship the buddha in your heart, not some printed materials. All the sutras are like roads that lead you to the realm of the saints. Don't hesitate to walk on these roads, even though you cherish them very much.

Someone told me I should chant the name of the Goddess of Mercy before noon, and Amitabha's name after noon. Is this appropriate?

It makes no difference, as long as you concentrate on chanting their names. You will enhance your compassion toward others by chanting the name of the Goddess of Mercy. You will increase your capacity for tolerance, trust and sense of open-mindedness by chanting Amitabha's name. By achieving a strong sense of tolerance, you will be able to acquire a great deal of good fortune. You will have a bright future if you are compassionate toward others.

I believe in the Buddha, and I often go to a temple to worship him and study his sutras. Should I do so every day?

It is not necessary. The fundamental way to show that you have faith in Buddhism is to demonstrate your determination to behave like the Buddha. You would not be a true Buddhist if you worshipped the Buddha yet did not act like him.

What is the difference between chanting "Sakyamuni" and "Amitabha"?

Sakyamuni is the fundamental teacher for Buddhists. We cultivate our morality in accordance with his teachings. Amitabha teaches us to forget all worldly concerns and to behold the Western World of Perfect Happiness ["Paradise"]. Actually, if we maintain tranquil minds, the whole world will also be pure.

I have heard the expression, "Be concerned as if you were not." What does it mean?

We should always be concerned about Buddha, not ourselves. And we should do this in a natural manner.

Will our problems be resolved if we beg the bodhisattvas for help?

Each human being has some kind of deep-seated worry according to his karma. If you pray devoutly to the bodhisattvas for help, they will mercifully show you the right way to eliminate your worries. If you accept Buddhist teachings, you will become stronger and more resolute. However, you should not always turn to Buddha for help when you are in trouble. The best way to overcome troubles is to be confident and resolute within yourself. Those are strengths you can always count on.

My husband disapproves of my worship of Buddha.

The worshipping of Buddha and chanting of sutras are merely methods to help us improve our character. Your family would certainly disapprove of your belief if you spent all your time chanting sutras in a temple, but continued to be stubborn and superstitious. Religion can enlighten us so that we can eliminate our egoism. After hearing your husband's complaints, you should re-examine your behavior from his point of view. This is the essence of love and the duty of a Buddhist.

Behaving Like Buddha

Why don't Buddhists talk about geomancy?

In Buddhism, we believe in the concept of karma, and there are two kinds of karma, good and bad. A person with good karma will find that wherever he goes, he will always be in a nice place. However, when a person has bad karma, he will not enjoy living in any particular place, even if that place is highly praised by a geomancer. So if you behave properly and always get along well with others, you will always have good fortune wherever you go.

How can we achieve a deep understanding of religion?

It is a goal that you cannot achieve within one or two days. Buddhism does not merely teach people to worship Buddha or perform Buddhist rituals. Actually, it teaches people to understand life, to get along with other people, and to explore the purpose of life.

Will belief in Buddhism damage family life?

Buddhism will never damage the happiness of families. It will never harm the love and romance between husband and wife. People can better cultivate virtue, manage the family, and help bring peace to the whole world by believing in Buddha and abiding by his precepts. Those who abide by Buddha's precepts are people with clear minds. They are warm and compassionate toward others.

Tzu Chi has become such a large organization, admired by hundreds of thousands of people. This would seem to be a sort of breakthrough in reforming Buddhism.

Many people say that I am reforming Buddhism, but actually I am reviving its old traditions. When Buddha was alive, he did not have any profound sutras to teach his disciples. He merely used the small things that happened around him as examples to teach people how to live happily, treat each other nicely, and devote their love to all living beings. He would also teach them by pointing out the impoverished living conditions, suffering and social problems of the people of India. I am acting in the same way as Buddha did some 2,500 years ago. So I am not reforming Buddhism, but I am doing what Buddha himself did.

Someone encouraged me to become a monk. However, I often have distracting thoughts and hear unreal sounds. I tried to get rid of them by chanting mantras, but the result was even worse.

It is not necessary for you to become a monk if you want to behave like Buddha. It will not do you any good to become a monk when you still have a lot of distracting thoughts. Some people try very hard to act like Buddha, treating their parents nicely, promoting Buddha's teachings, and so forth. These people are not monks or nuns, but they successfully achieve their goal of imitating Buddha's good behavior. They are what we call "domestic bodhisattvas." Buddhism is a lively yet relaxing religion, but we must believe in true Buddhism. You should refrain from meditating and chanting mantras unless you have found a good instructor. And you should turn a deaf ear to the unreal sounds. They will eventually fade. The sounds you hear are, in fact, your own mental attachments.

Master, you seldom use abstruse words when preaching Buddha's philosophy, yet your words are very appealing and convincing.

The importance of Buddha's teachings is not their profundity. They simply teach us how to live happy, meaningful lives. Buddha's teachings are closely connected to our lives. This was Buddha's concept of religion.

How can we understand Buddha's teachings?

You should learn from Buddha's teachings as much as possible, dwell upon them, live by them and, above all, put them into practice. After doing all this, you will understand Buddha's teachings. You will then be wiser and free from worry.

Unselfish Giving

Why do rich people seldom do good deeds?

Rich people usually lack a strong desire to unselfishly give what they have to others. It is also difficult for them to limit their worldly desires or to offer their love and compassion to other living creatures. This is because they fail to perceive the truth of life. For this reason, it is difficult for them to cultivate virtue or do good deeds.

If I make a lot of money on the stock market, I will donate a large part of my profit to Tzu Chi.

We do not have a penny when we come into this world, and we will not take a penny with us when we leave. You would do better to earn your money in a regular way and donate it according to your financial ability. Do not let your emotions fluctuate in accordance with the ups and downs of the share price index. If I advised you not to invest in the stock exchange, you would surely thank me when the index falls, but you would also surely complain to me when it goes up. How can you cultivate your wisdom when your mood fluctuates according to stock market changes? How can you have enough energy to work on other matters? You will have an unencumbered mind when you decide not to earn money this way.

It's very difficult to earn money, so I am not so stupid as to share what I have earned with others.

You should share what you have earned with other people. We should sow the seeds of kindness while we can today, so that we can reap rewards and blessings in the future. Which is more stupid, to help others while you can or to create bad karma for yourself by hoarding every penny in a bank? It is a big mistake when you assume that you are smart but do no good for other people.

Moral Cultivation

We often use the phrase "one thousand hands and one thousand eyes" to describe the capabilities of the bodhisattvas. What is the significance of this?

The "thousand hands and eyes" is a metaphor for completeness. With one thousand eyes, you can see the suffering of all living creatures, and with one thousand hands, you can reach out to help them.

How can we go to the Western World of Perfect Happiness?

You must be determined to act like a bodhisattva and cultivate kindness and good fortune in order to reach that goal. You also need to put your good ideas into practice by taking action. The distance between the Western Pure Land and the world we live in is too far to be measured. We cannot reach paradise without practicing good deeds.

Can one better help all living creatures by becoming a monk or nun?

Being a monk or nun is a great mission, and you need to cultivate a healthy mind first. When you become a monk or nun, you should not immediately begin to spread Buddha's teachings and help all living creatures. You should first learn how to set yourself free from worry and get along well with the other monks and nuns.

I want to teach primary school students how to behave properly in the hope that they will not commit any crimes when they grow up. Please tell me how I can best fulfill this task.

You must cherish your own happy family and carefully educate your own children. It is also appropriate for you to take the time to act as a volunteer safety guard at your children's school or at the nursery school in your community. Try to make friends with children. You will then be able to show your love and wisdom to them.

It is such a tough job to help the poor. There are so many that we can never help them all. It worries me to think of this.

It is natural for a kind person like you to sympathize with those in trouble and offer them help. However, even the Buddha could not deliver all living creatures. We can only do our best to help them whenever possible.

The Diamond Sutra says, "One cannot cling to the concepts of being and non-being." What does this mean?

One should not cling to these two concepts. One should adopt the rule of the golden mean and keep these concepts in balance. If a balancing scale is off balance, it will fall down. The words printed on a page of a book are only a false image that will soon disappear [non-being]. However, we must rely on these false images to arrive at the essential truth that they contain [being]. If we keep our principles and our daily actions in balance, then our lives will not lose direction. Therefore, we must not cling to either "being" or "non-being."

A member asked about the importance of actions in the process of imitating Buddha's behavior.

Buddha was a holy man with both good fortune and wisdom. If we want to have Buddha's good fortune and wisdom, we must cultivate them by performing practical actions as a way to implement our good intentions to help all living creatures. As I often say, to become as good as Buddha is our goal as ordinary people. Buddha himself was an ordinary person when he started. However, we must walk on the Path of the Bodhisattvas and perform actions that are beneficial to all living creatures in order to reach our final goal — becoming a buddha.

If a person is thinking about becoming a monk or nun, what kind of mentality should he or she have?

Try to serve human beings with a positive mentality. You must first fully understand the spirit of Buddhism before you determine whether or not you are suitable to become a monk or nun.

People suffer because of the bad karma that they create by doing evil deeds. Can we prevent these people from doing bad things by explaining Buddha's teachings to them?

Buddhist masters have been continually spreading Buddha's teachings. They help correct people's minds, pull out the roots of their mistakes and so prevent them from doing bad things. If the karmic conditions are right, people will naturally hear and practice Buddha's teachings.

Physical fatigue does not bother me at all. But what I really can't stand is the friction between people I work with.

If you want to walk on the Path of the Bodhisattvas, you must not be afraid to face difficulties or challenges, whether physical or mental. You can only achieve the goal of becoming a good person like Buddha by enduring all the friction between people. Don't quit when you face problems. To Buddha, everyone is entitled to become enlightened. What worries Buddha is that we might lose our fervor on our way to enlightenment.

It is the duty of us disciples to serve Buddha, his teachings, and the communities of monks and nuns. But you refuse to let us serve you. Do you think you could be preventing us from obtaining the good fortune we would earn by serving you?

There are three ways to serve your master: with money, respect and action. How would it be possible for a Buddhist nun like me to fulfill the four missions of the Tzu Chi Foundation without your financial support? It is much more significant for you to financially support my commitments, which will remain after I am gone, than to help my mortal body. All the commissioners of Tzu Chi have regarded my missions as their own. This is "serving with respect." Furthermore, you can work together to help the poor and educate the rich, thus putting your commitments into action on the Path of the Bodhisattvas. This is "serving with action." If you can perform all three ways of serving, I would indeed be a master fully served by her disciples.

Why do we prostrate ourselves before the Master?

All devotees need to pay respect to the three Buddhist treasures of Buddha, his teachings and the congregations of monks and nuns. All monks and nuns help spread Buddha's teachings. If you cannot outwardly show your respect for them, how can you sincerely accept what they preach?

What does "Amitabha" mean?

It means infinite life, light and wisdom. Therefore, the word contains many blessings.

A husband of one of our members has not yet converted to Buddhism, because he is worried that other people might say he was redeemed by his wife.

It is good to be redeemed by someone else. "To redeem" means that you influence others by using personal examples of moral uprightness. You can only achieve this by first correcting your own mistaken ways.

What does "unrecognized good deeds" mean?

You should not expect other people to be aware of all the,good deeds you perform. Just be concerned about being helpful.

We sometimes perform meritorious deeds on behalf of someone who is dead. What is the meaning of this?

You should sincerely want to do something for the dead. Both the doer and the dead will be blessed. The living will obtain the reward for the meritorious deed, while the dead will receive the merits for having contributed their love to the world and for bringing you to Buddhism.

Is there a lot of difference between people who believe in Buddha and those who do not believe?

There is not much difference between the two, just as there is not much difference between Buddha's nature and human nature. A major difference, though, exists between people who behave like Buddha and those who do not. The former are people who do this-worldly affairs with an other-worldly spirit and who never succumb to difficulties. They sacrifice their own interests if necessary, and so they are not concerned about personal losses and gains. As for those who do not behave like Buddha, they care very much about what they gain and lose. We can say that the major difference between these two groups of people lies in their religious conviction: that is, to live for nothing other than the well-being of all living creatures.

Why do Buddhists stress the importance of chanting Buddha's name for the benefit of people who are dying?

When a person is dying, his nerves are about to fail. It is a painful moment in the life of the patient. We can help him feel less unhappy by chanting Buddha's name. Also, the sound of our voices will help his spirit concentrate in order to resist the temptations of evil ghosts.

There are quite a few bodhisattvas, but why do most people like to worship the Goddess of Mercy?

This is because the Goddess of Mercy has a more intimate relationship with living creatures. She is especially able to hear the laments of living creatures. Although living creatures can endure their pain, they feel relieved when receiving the care and concern of someone compassionate. This goddess is certainly compassionate. That is why people feel close to her.

It is so difficult to cultivate virtue. I have encountered a lot of setbacks. What should I do?

Try to understand Buddha's teachings thoroughly. However, you should not take worldly human affairs too seriously. We work with ordinary people every day, and of course we will face disagreements. Though we might become upset by these things, we should learn to remain calm in our deepest heart. So, don't quit. Try as best you can to walk on the Path of the Bodhisattvas.

A secular Buddhist [one who cultivates morality in the daily world] asked, "How can people like me eliminate our attachment to a particular cause or idea?"

Any secular Buddhist who wants to cultivate virtue must first cultivate his mind. If a secular Buddhist does not let go of all his attachments, his ignorance and worries will interfere with his moral cultivation. If you always think of your attachments, it will be difficult for you to eliminate your worries.

Is the Ghost-Feeding Festival a Buddhist or Taoist festival? Or, is it a folk religion festival? Also, is it against Buddha's philosophy to celebrate this festival in an extravagant way?

In Buddhism, it is called the Ullambana Festival [similar to the Christian All Souls Day]. Ullambana is a Sanskrit word meaning "to hang upside-down," which refers to the extreme suffering of the Hungry Ghosts in hell. Their throats are as slim as needles, so they cannot swallow any amount of food. We often offer food for the purpose of releasing from hell the souls of those who have died. A good Buddhist should have a deep understanding of this festival. Do not waste your time and energy on meaningless, extravagant rituals. Otherwise, you will misunderstand the Buddhist virtue of thrift.

How can I cultivate contemplation?

Make mental concentration a habit. Once you can fully concentrate your mind, you can cultivate your ability to contemplate.

A member asked about the right way to repent.

Let bygones be bygones. Don't repeat the same mistakes in the future. Seize the day so you can do as many good deeds as possible.

"I have seen many temples in Taiwan," a foreign visitor said. "The temple at the Abode of Still Thoughts is one of few that does not have exquisite carvings, beautiful statues of Buddha or colorful decorations. It is, in fact, very simple and plain. What do you intend to preserve or eliminate by this?"

"We want to preserve Buddha's spirit and eliminate the material comforts of life."

"Since Buddha's spirit dwells in our mind and our behavior," the visitor continued, "why do so many religious groups still practice their formal rituals?"

"The invisible religious spirit is often manifested through rituals. The reason we human beings are different from other animals is because we have developed various kinds of ceremonies to express our beliefs. They cannot be abolished."

Karmic Hindrances

What are karmic hindrances?

Sometimes a person prevents you from doing something you intended to do. He obstructs you because you did the same thing to him once before in a previous life. The bad deeds committed in the past created a bad karma. This sort of preventive action is what we call a karmic hindrance.

Someone said women have more karmic hindrances than men. Is this correct?

Not necessarily. A woman's strength will become great if she is truly determined. Avalokitesvara Bodhisattva is a good example. He often came into the world in the female form of the Goddess of Mercy. How compassionate a woman's heart can be! Compassion breeds wisdom, and you can then help promote the work of saving the world. A woman should not underestimate herself.

After learning meditation, a once shy and melancholy boy often spoke of achieving immortality. The 10-year-old's concerned parents took the child to see the Master.

The illusions in your mind are like the images on a TV screen. You see them when you switch on your mental TV. It would be better for an energetic young man like you to take part in more outdoor activities. Try to get closer to the natural environment. You can accumulate a lot of misconceptions if you lock yourself in a room and meditate all day long. Only a healthy body can bring you a healthy life. You will live an empty life if you only care about things that do not exist.

What is the "evil way"?

We often see a person who appears to have acquired a lot of wisdom after cultivating himself with Buddhist practices and yet still cannot eliminate all the attachments and worries in his heart. That is the "evil way."

What are "mental poisons"?

They are greed and anger. In this world, we often find these poisons because people are selfish. Their greed produces anger. When a person is angry, he hurts all living creatures.

Becoming a Buddhist

A member asked about the significance of becoming a Buddhist.

It means that a person forsakes darkness for light. Before he becomes a Buddhist, his heart is filled with dark thoughts. Afterwards, he progresses in the bright side of life, eliminating all his faults, acting with proper diligence and prudence, and resolutely and bravely carrying out the goodness, beauty and truth of life.

As Buddha's disciples, we should be as compassionate as Buddha. Though we might have once been rude to each other, even throwing things at each other when feeling offended, we should now correct all such mistakes. Try to treat others with an accommodating and loving heart. The significance of becoming a Buddhist lies not in obtaining Buddha's blessings, but in cultivating a heart that is full of love and sincerity and making the Buddha's compassion our own.